collective
BRIGHTNESS

LGBTIQ Poets on Faith, Religion & Spirituality

edited by Kevin Simmonds

SiblingRivalryPress

Alexander, Arkansas
www.siblingrivalrypress.com

Sibling Rivalry Press, LLC
13913 Magnolia Glen Drive
Alexander, AR 72002

ISBN: 978-0-9832931-9-4

Library of Congress Control Number: 2011931804

First Sibling Rivalry Press Edition, October 2011
Second Sibling Rivalry Press Edition, January 2012

The mission of Sibling Rivalry Press is to develop, publish, and promote outlaw
artistic talent — those projects which inspire people to read, challenge, and
ponder the complexities of life in dark rooms, under blankets by cell-phone
illumination, in the backseats of cars, and on spring-day park benches next to
people reading Lucille Clifton and Walt Whitman. We welcome manuscripts
which push boundaries, sing sweetly, or inspire us to perform karaoke in drag.
Not much makes us flinch.

For more information, visit us online.

www.siblingrivalrypress.com

contents

Dear Reader,

These poems, all of them, are for you.

introduction

These poems are the creations of poets who move through this world so variously that, taken collectively, one must brace for the illuminated brilliance of even the smallest thing. When I conceived the idea for this anthology, I had a hunch these poems existed but could never have imagined their scope. And I'm not merely referring to the many religions, faiths, spiritualities, belief and non-belief systems represented. I'm also talking about the uncountable ways poets interpreted my call for the anthology, sharing both real and imagined experiences, and how dizzyingly observed those experiences are expressed.

I grew up Catholic (I was an altar boy), had a conversion experience in high school and lived, for several years, as a Fundamentalist Christian. During those years, I didn't want to see beyond my own certainty, my own modes of belief I thought would protect me. When it became clear I couldn't be truly safe that way, I began moving through what often seems like a determinedly dark world, *without* a fixed certainty. Rather, I have come to prefer faith, which religion scholar Karen Armstrong refers to as the "opposite of certainty." Abiding with this faith, however, is one very personal certainty: No matter what, as a gay man, I belong.

Many LGBTIQ people have fought to feel ease and belonging when talking about faith, religion and spiritual issues. They have faced devastating rejection, shame, castigation and scapegoating for being themselves and loving as they do. Loving. Imagine that profound irony. Love, the one undeniably shared fundamental of all organized religions is the very reason for this *disease*. And if we are all, in fact, one body fanning out into different races, creeds, faiths, religions, spiritualities, philosophies and strivings, this *disease* is debilitating, not just for selected parts, but grave for the whole.

This is the first anthology in which LGBTIQ poets, over 100 of them, claim their place — in every territory and dominion, on earth, below it, above it, in the seen and unseen, the past, the present and future eternity — regardless of man-made labels or boundaries. Content dictates form and, thus, these poems are neither categorized nor ordered in any way. Instead, they appear in unpredictable patterns given the poets' surnames. While mood, expression and form vary from page to page just as religion, denomination, rite and practice do, the insistent light never dims.

As editor, I corresponded frequently with these poets and translators and learned some about how their lives impact their work and their work impacts their lives.

Foremost in my mind from the collection of fascinating and inspiring stories is how I came to know Azwan Ismail. In December 2010 he posted a YouTube video for the *It Gets Better Project* (TM), a campaign started by the columnist and author

Dan Savage to, among other things, rally around LGBT youth and encourage them to look forward to their lives as openly gay adults. Azwan, a writer and engineer based in Kuala Lumpur, recorded his video in the Malay language and, within days, received death threats for "promoting" homosexuality. Earlier that year, he edited *Orang Macam Kita*, Malaysia's first Malay-language LGBT anthology.

Seeing the video shortly after its posting, I contacted Azwan through his publisher, Matahari Books, about contributing to this anthology. The following day, he responded with interest but it would take another two months for him to reply to my subsequent emails. When he finally responded, he apologized and explained that it had taken so long for things to die down a bit. This is the first time his work has appeared in English.

There are other firsts: According to Gabriel Sylvian, a scholar in the field of Korean literature and translator of Seung-Ja Choe (최승자), this marks the first time that a Korean poet appears in an LGBTIQ anthology of any kind. Despite having written actively for over twenty years and being an important poet in Japan, Atsusuke Tanaka (田中宏輔) has only recently come to the attention of the English-speaking world. This is the first time his work has appeared in English by way of award-winning Japanese translator Jeffrey Angles.

Another first, for me, was being completely unable to contact a poet for several consecutive months. Award-winning London poet and writer Maitreyabandhu was on retreat. He is a Buddhist monk.

Poet and teacher Ellen Bass, whose excitement for poetry is contagious, generously and enthusiastically shared her knowledge with me during the process. Benjamin S. Grossberg's poem "Beetle Orgy" gifted me with the anthology's luminous title. And Bryan Borland, the force behind Sibling Rivalry Press, dared me to maintain my vision as he backed me — without fail — every single step of the way.

Collective Brightness features established and emerging poets from around the world. Yet I hesitate to say that it is representative of anything other than my attempt to gather, for the first time in one volume, gifted LGBTIQ poets writing from more than a single spiritual or religious purview, collectively aiding seekers of all kinds to experience and withstand the weight of love shining.

One love,

Kevin Simmonds
San Francisco, June 2011

collective
BRIGHTNESS

FRANKLIN ABBOTT

Koan

my face
before my birth
was half
my father's face
looking
back into
eternity
the half-him
that was me
fought countless wars
loved myriad women
sired a thousand sons
a thousand daughters

I am the end of all that
I am fruit ripening
with no seed to plant
no progeny to offer
a crowded world
my gift is who I am
outside of history
facing time dissolving
in an ever present moment
with gentle men
whose loving
knows no purpose
but to kindle
in our hearts
the quiet light
of peace

KAZIM ALI

Home

My father had a steel comb with which he would comb our hair.

After a bath the cold metal soothing against my scalp, his hand cupping my chin.

My mother had a red pullover with a little yellow duck embroidered on it and a pendant made from a gold Victoria coronation coin.

Which later, when we first moved to Buffalo, would be stolen from the house.

The Sunn'i Muslims have a story in which the angels cast a dark mark out of Prophet Mohammad's heart, thus making him pure, though the Shi'a reject this story, believing in his absolute innocence from birth.

Telling the famous Story of the Blanket in which the Prophet covers himself with a Yemeni blanket for his afternoon rest. Joined under the blanket first by his son-in-law Ali, then each of his grandchildren Hassan and Hussain and finally by his daughter Bibi Fatima.

In Heaven Gabriel asks God about the five under the blanket and God says, those are the five people whom I loved the most out of all creation, and I made everything in the heavens and the earth for their sake.

Gabriel, speaker on God's behalf, whisperer to Prophets, asks God, can I go down and be the sixth among them.

And God says, go down there and ask them. If they consent you may go under the blanket and be the sixth among them.

Creation for the sake of Gabriel is retroactively granted when the group under the blanket admits him to their company.

Is that me at the edge of the blanket asking to be allowed inside.

Asking the 800 *hadith* be canceled, all history re-ordered.

In Hyderabad I prayed every part of the day, climbed a thousand steps to the site of Maula Ali's pilgrimage.

I wanted to be those stairs, the hunger I felt, the river inside.

I learned to pronounce my daily prayers from transliterated English
in a book called "Know Your Islam," dark blue with gold calligraphed
writing that made the English appear as if it were Arabic complete with
marks above and below the letters.

I didn't learn the Arabic script until years later and never learned the
language itself.

God's true language: Hebrew. Latin. Arabic. Sanskrit.

As if utterance fit into the requirements of the human mouth.

I learned how to find the new moon by looking for the circular absence
of stars.

When Abraham took Isaac up into the thicket his son did not know
where he was being led.

When his father bound him and took up the knife he was shocked.

And said, "Father, where is the ram?"

Though from Abraham's perspective he was asked by God to sacrifice
his son and proved his love by taking up the knife.

Thinking to himself perhaps, Oh Ismail, Ismail, do I cut or do I burn.

I learned God's true language is only silence and breath.

Fourth son of a fourth son, my father was afflicted as a child and
as was the custom in those days a new name was selected for him to
protect his health.

Still the feeling of his rough hand, gently cupping my cheek, dipping the
steel comb in water to comb my hair flat.

My hair was kept so short, combed flat when wet. I never knew my hair
was wavy until I was nearly twenty-two and never went outside with wet
and uncombed hair until I was twenty-eight.

At which point I realized my hair was curly.

My father's hands have fortune-lines in them cut deeply and dramatic.

The day I left his house for the last time I asked him if I could hold his hand before I left.

There are two different ways of going about this.
If you have known this for years why didn't you ask for help, he asked me.

Each time I left home, including the last time, my mother would hold a Quran up for me to walk under. Once under, one would turn and kiss the book.

There is no place in the Quran which requires acts of homosexuality to be punishable by lashings and death.

Hadith or scripture. Scripture or rupture.

Should I travel out from under the blanket.

Comfort from a verse which also recurs: "Surely there are signs in this for those of you who would reflect."

Or the one hundred and four books of God. Of which only four are known — *Qur'an, Injeel, Tavrat, Zubuur.*

There are a hundred others — *Bhagavad-Gita, Lotus Sutra, Song of Myself, the Gospel of Magdalene, Popul Vuh, the book of Black Buffalo Woman* — somewhere unrevealed as such.

Dear mother in the sky you could unbuckle the book and erase all the annotations.

What I always remember about my childhood is my mother whispering to me, telling me secrets, ideas, suggestions.

She named me when I moved in her while she was reading a calligraphy of the Imam's names. My name: translated my whole life for me as Patience.

In India we climbed the steps of the Maula Ali mountain to the top, thirsting for what.

My mother had stayed behind in the house, unable to go on pilgrimage. She had told me the reason why.

Being in a state considered unacceptable for prayers or pilgrimages.

I asked if she would want more children and she told me the name she would give a new son.

I always attribute the fact that they did not, though my eldest sister's first son was given the same name she whispered to me that afternoon, to my telling of her secret to my sisters when we were climbing the stairs.

It is the one betrayal of her — perhaps meaningless — that I have never forgiven myself.

There are secrets it is still hard to tell, betrayals hard to make.

You hope like anything that though others consider you unclean God will still welcome you.

My name is Kazim. Which means *patience*. I know how to wait.

SHIRLETTE AMMONS

Roberta is Working Clergy

Roberta works the Savior's packing line
pearled in purple choir curtains and citrus sponge curlers
she and The Word perch on slaughtering surfaces
slaying Satan and singeing curt breathing from early cocks
Roberta is The Blood, The Way, The Water

In the break room,
Lance chips and honey buns wait with TD Jakes
Roberta binds the sweets in thin slices of Scripture,
gurgles, urgently, her nurturing need, *Lord,*
Have Mercy on your working Durga, she pleads;

Bosses, *Hell-bound Heathens,* she calls them,
mimic her calling, curse her unskilled altar
yet, they gather, the fishes and the loaves,
at the feet of her cock-slit pulpit
eager to be dismantled,
like the gizzard from the giblet,
The Word, their perfect minimum wage

Before break time unburdens its serpents,
lurking with demerits & demotions,
The Spirit splays like disobedient turkey gall
she stays, Rahab amidst the loosened walls of Jericho,
to gird the Unlearned hurrying to The Promised Land

Roberta benedicts the persecuted,
from God's forgone turf, they disperse
on the brink of the briny Jordan
the scarlet rope saves her page,
she approaches the throne of Herod
to receive her scalding
burning in faith for tomorrow's crossing

CHRISSY ANDERSON-ZAVALA

The cross

On the border between Tecate and Centro
power lines crackle and buzz overhead
like flies swarming under our eyelids;
boulders transform to skulls that chatter
and stare and say nothing. East of Tecate,
Border Patrol agents perch atop sandstone
mountains, all quiet gleaming steel. The soil
gathers — clandestine — in our nostrils.

Bullet holes mock religious wanderers;
this is not desert. Twelve times, Jesus has died here,
trying to find reprieve.

Salvation

speak of angels suspended on
the shoulders of single mothers
as their shifts end kids in bed
speak to me of the god who cradles
the bodies of young girls as they find
desire in that same flesh
speak of a hellfire reserved
for beer breath ripping the cloth
of a woman as she cries out to a god
who does not come

speak to me of a place to lay tired limbs
where the skin of eager lovers peals away
like husks arching back in awe of the dark
luminescent kernels
speak to me in liberation's tongue
in the smooth green arms of aloe
in the curl of dual spines

speak to me of the god with sore feet
worn boots mud-caked and leaning
while the stove's flame tickles the comal
and will rise when we rise

ARI BANIAS

To the God of Sobriety

You don't even have to say it:
                  What would happen if instead
        of tumbling into another drink —
    as if into the salt skin of a new boy — the fall
into the swirled idea of what is possible in the unknown jangling dark

I admit it: I already know. I know
    the way his bed will groan
    dirty socks in the corner. Know the
      well-kept plants breathing lightly
          in the window like shrines to being alive.

Know air so dry whatever's spilled
is gone by afternoon. I know gum drained of all flavor
          riding the ghosts of six rum & cokes. I know
            the bliss is quick, & not bliss
& the next day's cracked
eternity a blister.

My options are few, but here *you* are, The Plain-Dressed One in the corner:
    presiding without seeming to, like an owl: unfazed-though-the-world's-
      falling down-around-you, yet so ordinary no one would ever know
        you're immortal —

And now you've brought me here
    & let me loose, where
        every surface glistens with sequined rivers of whiskey
        to see what I'll do?

    it's tempting, but really —
the more time I spend with you the more
you keep unplugging the world. You've invited me

      softly around the back, shown me the tangle
        of wires and switches & the piling up

    junk drawer of being alive: rubber bands,
toothpicks, soy sauce packets, pennies. Those twisty-ties! How can I go back?
I've got to get as far
away as possible from what I know:

You make it so I can't not knock
the frame that's always hung there
off the wall   and find the punched-in hole.

I can't refuse.
Your invitation goes blowing & stripping
& burning its gentle way through me

like a benevolent storm.   It's still raining but *bring it*. I just got home.

Some Kind of We

These churchbells bong out
one to another in easy conversation
a pattern, a deep ringing that wants to say
things are okay,
things are okay —
but things, they are not okay
I can't trust a churchbell, though I would like to
the way I can trust
that in this country, in every house and in most every
apartment, there somewhere is a cabinet or drawer
where it's stashed, the large plastic bag
with slightly smaller mashed together plastic bags inside it;
it is overflowing, and we keep adding,
bringing home more than we need, we should have
to weave a three piece suit of plastic bags
a rug, a quilt, a bed of bags even, anything
more useful than this collection this excess
why am I writing about plastic bags, because
it is this year in this country and I am this person
with this set of meanings on my body and the majority of what I have,
I mean, what I literally have the most of in my apartment, more
than plants, more than forks and spoons and knives combined, more than chairs
or jars or pens or books or socks, is plastic bags,
and I am trying to write, generally and specifically,
through what I see and what I know,
about my life (about our lives?),
if in all this there can still be — tarnished,
problematic, and certainly uneven — a *we*.

ELLEN BASS

Pray for Peace

Pray to whomever you kneel down to:
Jesus nailed to his wooden or plastic cross,
his suffering face bent to kiss you,
Buddha still under the bo tree in scorching heat,
Adonai, Allah. Raise your arms to Mary
that she may lay her palm on our brows,
to Shekinah, Queen of Heaven and Earth,
to Inanna in her stripped descent.

Then pray to the bus driver who takes you to work.
On the bus, pray for everyone riding that bus,
for everyone riding buses all over the world.
Drop some silver and pray.

Waiting in line for the movies, for the ATM,
for your latte and croissant, offer your plea.
Make your eating and drinking a supplication.
Make your slicing of carrots a holy act,
each translucent layer of the onion, a deeper prayer.

To Hawk or Wolf, or the Great Whale, pray.
Bow down to terriers and shepherds and Siamese cats.
Fields of artichokes and elegant strawberries.

Make the brushing of your hair
a prayer, every strand its own voice,
singing in the choir on your head.
As you wash your face, the water slipping
through your fingers, a prayer: Water,
softest thing on earth, gentleness
that wears away rock.

Making love, of course, is already prayer.
Skin, and open mouths worshipping that skin,
the fragile cases we are poured into.

If you're hungry, pray. If you're tired.
Pray to Gandhi and Dorothy Day.
Shakespeare. Sappho. Sojourner Truth.

When you walk to your car, to the mailbox,
to the video store, let each step
be a prayer that we all keep our legs,
that we do not blow off anyone else's legs.
Or crush their skulls.
And if you are riding on a bicycle
or a skateboard, in a wheelchair, each revolution
of the wheels a prayer as the earth revolves:
less harm, less harm, less harm.

And as you work, typing with a new manicure,
a tiny palm tree painted on one pearlescent nail,
or delivering soda or drawing good blood
into rubber-capped vials, twirling pizzas —

With each breath in, take in the faith of those
who have believed when belief seemed foolish,
who persevered. With each breath out, cherish.

Pull weeds for peace, turn over in your sleep for peace,
feed the birds, each shiny seed
that spills onto the earth, another second of peace.
Wash your dishes, call your mother, drink wine.

Shovel leaves or snow or trash from your sidewalk.
Make a path. Fold a photo of a dead child
around your Visa card. Scoop your holy water
from the gutter. Gnaw your crust.
Mumble along like a crazy person, stumbling
your prayer through the streets.

God and the G-Spot

He didn't want to believe. He wanted to know.
   - Ann Druyan, Carl Sagan's wife, on why he didn't believe in God

I want to know too. Belief and disbelief
are a pair of tourists standing on swollen feet
in the Prado — *I don't like it.*
I do. — before the Picasso.

Or the tattoo artist with a silver stud
in her full red executive lips,
who, as she inked in the indigo blue, said,
I think the G-spot's one of those myths
men use to make us feel inferior.

God, the G-spot, falling in love. The earth round
and spinning, the galaxies speeding
in the glib flow of the Hubble expansion.
I'm an East Coast Jew. We all have our opinions.

But it was in the cabin at La Selva Beach
where I gave her the thirty tiny red glass hearts
I'd taken back from my husband when I left.
He'd never believed in them. She, though, scooped
them up like water, let them drip through her fingers
like someone who has so much she can afford to waste.

That's the day she reached inside me
for something I didn't think I had.
And like pulling a fat shining trout from the river
she pulled the river out of me. That's
the way I want to know God.

Ode to The God of Atheists

The god of atheists won't burn you at the stake
or pry off your fingernails. Nor will it make you
bow or beg, rake your skin with thorns,
or buy gold leaf and stained-glass windows.
It won't insist you fast or twist
the shape of your sexual hunger.
There are no wars fought for it, no women stoned for it.
You don't have to veil your face for it
or bloody your knees.
You don't have to sing.

The plums that bloom extravagantly,
the dolphins that stitch sky to sea,
each pebble and fern, pond and fish
are yours whether or not you believe.

When fog is ripped away
just as a rust red thumb slides across the moon,
the god of atheists isn't rewarding you
for waking up in the middle of the night
and shivering barefoot in the field.

This god is not moved by the musk
of incense or bowls of oranges,
the mask brushed with cochineal,
polished rib of the lion.
Eat the macerated leaves
of the sacred plant. Dance
till the stars blur to a spangly river.
Rain, if it comes, will come.
This god loves the virus as much as the child.

God's Grief

Great parent
who must have started out
with such high hopes.
What magnitude of suffering,
the immensity of guilt,
the staggering despair.
A mind the size of the sun,
burning with longing,
a heart huge as a gray whale
breaching, streaming
seawater against the pale sky.
Man god or beast god,
god that breathes in every pleated leaf,
throat sac of frog, pinfeather and shaft —
god of plutonium and penicillin, drunk
sleeping on the subway grate,
god of Joan of Arc, god of Crazy Horse,
Lady Day, bringing us to our knees,
god of Houdini with hands
like a river, of Einstein, regret
running thick in his veins,
god of Stalin, god of Somoza,
god of the long march,
the Trail of Tears,
the trains,
god of Allende and god of Tookie,
the strawberry picker, fire in his back,
god of midnight, god of winter,
god of rouged children sold
with a week's lodging
and airfare to Thailand,
god in trouble, god at the end of his rope —
sleepless, helpless —
desperate god, frantic god, whale heart
lost in the shallows, beached
on the sand, parched, blistered, crushed
by gravity's massive weight.

JEFFERY BEAM

St. Jerome in His Study

after Dürer

There is a jar
buried beneath the cloister
with five words I have
kept in my pocket
all my life

solitude and wisdom
light and virtue and
a shadow of pain with thick lips
drinking from a cup

Once   in the gardens
I watched a sparrow
carry a blue silence
to the mountains

It was a rosy sorrow
I caught there
an underground rolling
of pure water
life's ever-
lasting dahlia
sacred

How the sunlight
sweetens the room
all I own written in the very boards
what I have given away
what comes to me

The mangled flesh
of fish
in a basket
A weaving staccato
watering my soul

The almond
a taste I will never forget
brown
beautifully simple

ROBIN BECKER

Quaker Meeting, The Sixties

Seeing my friend's son in his broad-brimmed hat
and suspenders, I think of the Quakers
who lectured us on nonviolent social action
every week when I was a child. In the classrooms
we listened to those would not take up arms,
who objected, who had accepted alternative
service in distant work camps and showed
slides of hospitals they helped to build.
On Wednesdays, in Meeting for Worship,
when someone rose to speak,
all the energy in the room
flew inside her mouth, empowering her to tell
what she had seen on her brief
encounter with the divine: sometimes, a parable,
a riddle, a kindness. The fall that we were seventeen,
we scuffed our loafers on the gravelly path
from the Meetinghouse, while maple and elm
leaves sailed around our shoulders
like tiny envelopes, our futures sealed inside.
Despite the war in Vietnam, I felt safer
than I ever would again. Perhaps
those aged, protective trees had cast a spell
on us, or maybe the nonviolent Quaker God
had set up a kingdom right there —
suburban Philadelphia. Looking back, I see how
good deeds and thoughts climbed with us to the attic
room for Latin, descended to the gym for sports,
where we hung from the praiseworthy scaffolds
of righteous behavior. We prepared to leave
for college, armed with the language of the American
Friends and the memories of Thanksgiving
dinners we'd cooked for the unfortunates:
borrowing our parents' cars to drive
downtown to the drop-off point, racing back
to play our last field hockey match. Grim center forwards
shook hands before the whistle, the half-backs'
knee-pads strapped on tight; one varsity team vanquished another.

Spiritual Morning

I am as virtuous as a rabbinical student
after my morning run, God in the body awake, God
of the May apple and wild ginger. Even the little
stiff hands of the whistle pig reach
toward me in the death's perfection. Once,
in Katmandu at dawn, I watched a monk in a saffron robe
brush his teeth on the roof of a temple and spit —
and from his mouth flew peach and azure birds
fluttering in the milky sweetness of the air.

      This morning of Pennsylvania
woodchuck and wild geranium, I grasp the
connection among all sentient beings and feel
communion with the wretched of all species and the dead.
The orange swallowtail looping overhead, for example,
is really my old grandmother, back to remind me
to learn Yiddish, the only international language.
I'd like her to sit on my finger
so we could talk face-to-face, but she flies
out of sight, shouting, *Big talker! Don't run on busy streets!*

DAN BELLM

Brand new

for Charlie Halloran

1

One of these mornings you're going to rise up singing —
Now Charlie's body is surrounded by
the work of his hands,
his hats and painted scarves
arrayed around him on the bed,
and on a tape from long ago he plays the flute
as we gather in the house — "Summertime"
in February light — All night he moaned
and vomited, sloughing off the body one agony
after another and his mind already at play somewhere,
talking to people we couldn't see in words
we couldn't hear until he stirred
a last time to come back — "hold me," he said,
and carefully David held his hands — he didn't much like
being touched any more — it hurt — "no, hold me,"
he said — so David lay beside him on the sheet
to cradle the sore bones and as one died
the other slept, worn out from the long night,
the work of love come to an end
and so much work undone.

2

In the middle of Joah's dance bowling balls
start careening across the stage, two or three
at first and it's more or less manageable to nudge them
off, even make a pleasing pattern of the interruption
and go on dancing, then it's happening much
faster than he can catch and guide them and at last
he has to give in and choose just one, set his fingers
inside and caress it, toss it into the air
and at its highest point the camera catches it
to make the photo next to Charlie's bed, Joah
gazing up in delight and unburdened after all
though he's long dead — the bowling ball
fell into his arms, and he lugged the weight away.

3

How do we forgive ourselves for what
we haven't done? The failures of courage
and heart, so much undared and un-
expressed — Over and over we talked about it,
the ways we hadn't measured up, done what
we'd told ourselves by now we would.
Charlie showed me once a little potted orchid
on his table, four pale blooms
like crumpled paper cups turned over — "the story
of my life," he said, trying to smile,
furious that day at what he'd given up on and have to
give up next, what would be taken away. First
the strength of his hands to sew and paint
and play music. Then his sight. Then his breath.
Then he did smile. "Fucking thing
only came this far and didn't open."
Taped to the wall is Adrienne's letter
urging, believing, "Yes,
you must continue," and what if our lives
are forgotten, and what if we're lost? We live on
in others but they will also die, and one day
it will be as if none of us had lived. I want to believe,
when everything that was given to us is taken
back, love remains, and won't forget.

4

Living without knowing, and every day
starting all over again — One day I saw him
on 18th Street, bundled in scarves
under the bright sun as if noon were
midnight and leaning at his cane and I moved
to kiss him until he snapped, "You can't do that,"
his voice gone harsh because
he'd had to say this now
too many times. Of course. I remember.
I can't kiss you any more. It was Pesach —
in the doctor's office he'd just approached the moment of death
in a waking dream, a spirit leading him to a wall
and to a door in the wall he had to open —
and there was a great cry in the land of Egypt,
for there was not a house where there was not one dead.
We had to begin again,
light the candles of the seder another year

and remember for each other the promise of freedom,
joining hands. Then Charlie read in the Haggadah
the voice of a child asking, "What good
will these rituals ever do for me?" and rushed away.
The orchids he had brought for the table
were a ritual, too, and as he cried
in the next room in his sister's arms
we looked at them,
ashamed of prayers made of words.

5

Hey babe: I greet you sitting in the sun
in your window seat, catching morning light,
threading tiny green beads on a string
to decorate your velvet hat: in the middle of the city
you're a bird of magic in the flowering branches
of a forest, impatient spirit, girl-boy, gay one,
beautiful and frail, with a button on your favorite cap
that says *Destination Unknown* — you're going out tonight
in rouge and a velvet dress and beaded hat
and the room's in a riot, sewing machines and hat blocks,
ironing boards and metal presses, wigs,
spray paint in cans, church hats for your nurses
from the hospital, spools of thread on pegs,
feathers and painted silk, shells and ribbons,
polished stones — You are home. You are transformed.
You tell me an angel spoke to you
when you were a child, telling you God is love,
the love of your family you will always have with you:
Hold fast to it and trust it and believe it.
Both our fathers think we've thrown away our faith now
and how can we explain we haven't turned away
but returned by different paths, fairy, pantheist, Jew,
because even though we're full of doubt
doubt dissatisfies us — *We praise the source of life*
who has kept us alive, and sustained us,
and brought us to this time. We're so old we're brand new.

Bo, Exodus 10:1-13:16

OLIVER BENDORF

The First Erasure[*]

for Matthew

god
may release hymns free
to the city

their shepard is not hate

has been 5.5 years
in his name

or a day

follow fire
the only way

a beautiful blue
one for each bearing
with this heavy mankind

matthew

october not granite
heavy

above words

---

[*]This poem was created through redaction of a fax sent by the Westboro Baptist Church, who carried signs that read "God Hates Fags" at the funeral of Matthew Shepard, and who also targeted me at my high school graduation.

AHIMSA TIMOTEO BODHRÁN

when i learned praying to be straight was not useful

the first time i brought a man to sweat, taught him to
offer tobacco, i came full circle. it is here i first lit fire.
and almost a decade later i return, with man. a year
later i returned, after the prayers had betrayed me,
after i had betrayed myself. and i tried not to judge
the man i brought with me. perhaps we always judge
those learning what we are ourselves. perhaps that is
what we offer the fire: to burn and renew, Ancestors
working through it for us in the flames. a year prior,
here, praying to be straight, praying to be anything
other than what i was: a lover of man. here i returned,
unalone, with family. i had not expected to be the
one teaching, guiding hand, voice, guiding body over
rock and stump, through kitchen, over stream by log,
snow flower, to a place where water falls, tumbling
over rock and cliff, into the first round, out the second,
sometimes all four, him still learning new lungs,
through the heat and dark, new breath.

something healed in me there. who knew in the loving
of another man, gentle, from a distance, i'd partake of
new waters, smell pine anew, count lichens of trees,
rejoice in swarmings of ladybugs on an evening shirt. who
knew i'd offer words to someone who didn't
know them, but heard them resonate in, quill, quiver,
from before birth. who knew i'd be teacher, and in
the teaching, taught: a new drum singing in my chest,
rhythm playing through our bodies, all the notes.

MOE BOWSTERN

I Give Up
a poem of surrender and gratitude

for John Rodgers

I had a friend —
Didn't we all? —
Who died of what we used to call AIDS
Remember that? "Full-blown AIDS"
He was an artist —
Weren't we all?

During his last winter I went to his apartment
Before Christmas
Helped construct what he called
"Crap to sell at the holiday fairs"
I was twenty-something, young for my age
I quailed in the company of his agony
Shrugged off his gratitude
Painted little homo angels with my head down,
Uncharacteristically monosyllabic.

After an hour or so he limped to the couch,
Laid down his cane,
Saying it was time
To give himself up to the cosmos.
He tried to do it every day.
"It's really hard," he said, on his back
Eyes closed
Arms out
Like the wooden homo angels I was painting.

This was Chicago in the 90s
We scorned Jesus Christ and horoscopes
We believed in winter, and in dancing
Balanced one against the other —
DeeLite, Monie Love, De La Soul —
We stayed alive by not dying.

Almost 20 years later I am in an open boat, in Alaska
Picking salmon from nets two or three times a day
The nets stay put; we go back and forth.
It's easier to think about the cosmos up here.

A humpback pulls in one day, puts on a show
Hear me say that, "puts on a show"
How fishermen speak, downplaying everything
As if time doesn't stop
When the Great Ones rear up

The humpback rises, impossible
Vertical levitation
The displaced ocean pours off its body
A waterfall from its open mouth

I hear the whale breathing
From fifty feet away
The air shimmers, sunlight skips on gray skin
My sudden tears,
The way I am holding my breath

I have fished now two decades, on and off
My boss twice that
The greenhorn is the first to speak.
"Wow!" he says, shattering the sanctity, "I've never seen that before!"
My boss and I exhale
"Me neither" we say in turn, "Me neither"
As the water erases the evidence
Of the cosmos.

The whale comes even closer after we leave
Tears through two of our three nets
Unzipped them
Leadline sinks to the bottom
Corkline and remaining web flutter on the surface
Where they snare a passing flock of murrelets
Tiny swimming birds

They struggled, many of them still alive
As we approach hours later, in the skiff
Dismayed, a sinking gut, yet
The beauty of the morning,
The whale
Dances still in our minds.

We concentrated on the live birds
Worked silently, our fingers clumsy
Handling fragile feet, wings, legs
Wrapped in monofilament.
Our monofilament.

Hunched over, gloves off
We commit the sin of cutting the meshes
To free the birds

We flip them on their backs
It's easier to see the clear web against the white breast feathers
And keeps them from drowning.
They strike us with their black beaks
Over and over, biting us
It's more startling than painful
"I'm sorry," I say,
As the birds gasp, and stab.

I save one, set it in the sea, reach for another
It's oddly like picking fish
From beyond the heaving handful
I catch glimpses of the survivors,
Paddling away on the tide

Their wingbeats on the water
Sound like applause,
Like forgiveness.

The others we bury in the garden.

Sometimes in my life
I get caught on the surface
Between Above and Below

I think of my friend, long dead
And I stretch out on the sofa,
Give myself up to the cosmos

The murrelets come to mind
A tiny bird on its back strikes at huge hands
That only want to help

Relax! Let go!
I will be freed!

From the couch, twenty years ago
I hear my friend's exhausted voice
"It's really hard."

ANA BOŽIĆEVIĆ

Death, Is All

I woke up real early to write about death (the lake through the trees) from
the angle of the angel. There's the kind of angel that when I say
Someone please push me out of the way
Of this bad poem like it was a bus. — well, it comes running &
tackles me and oh, it's divine football — Or
in the dream when the transparent buses
came barreling towards us: — it was there. Half of all Americans say

they believe in angels. And why shouldn't they.
If someone swoops in to tell them how death's a fuzzy star that's
full of bugles, well it's a hell of a lot better
than what they see on TV: the surf much too warm for December, and roller
coasters full of the wounded and the subconscious
that keep pulling in — Who wants to believe

death's just another life inside a box, tale-pale or more vivid?
Not me. Like in *Gladiator*, when they showed the cypresses
flanking the end-road — O set
Your sandal, your tandem bike, into the land of shadows — of course
I cried. Show me a cypress and I'll just go off, but
I don't want *that* to be it. Or
some kind of poem you can never find your way out of! And sometimes

I think I nod at the true death: when from a moving train
I see a house in the morning sun
and it casts a shadow on the ground, an inquiry
and I think "Crisp inquiry"
& go on to work, perfumed of it — that's the kind of death
I'm talking about.

An angle of light. Believe in it. I believe in the light and disorder of the word
repeated until quote Meaning unquote leeches out of it. And that's
what I wanted to do with dame Death, for you:
repeat it until you're all, What? D-E-A-T-H! 'Cause Amy
that's all it is, a word, material in the way the lake through the trees
is material, that is: insofar, not at all.
Because we haven't yet swam in it. See what I mean?
I see death, I smell death, it moves the hair on my face but

I don't know where it blows from. And in its sources is my power.
I'm incredibly powerful in my ignorance. I'm incredible, like some kind of fuzzy star.

The nonsense of me is the nonsense of death, and
Oh look! Light through the trees on the lake:

the lake has the kind of calmness
my pupils' surface believes . . . and this is just the thing
that the boxed land of shades at the end of the remote
doesn't program for: the lake is so kind to me, Amy,
and I'll be so kind to you, Amy, and so we'll never die:
there'll be plenty of us around to
keep casting our inquiry
against the crisp light. Light is all like,
what's up, I'm here I'm an angel! & we're
all: no you're not, that doesn't exist. We all laugh and laugh . . .

Or cry and cry. The point is, it's words, and so's
death. Even in that silence
there's bird calls or meteors or something hurtling
through space: there's matter and light. I've seen it
through the theater of the trees and it was beautiful

It cut my eyes and I didn't even care

I already had the seeing taken care of. Even in the months I didn't have
a single poem in me, I had this death and this love, and how's
that not enough? I even have a quote:
Love is the angel

Which leads us into the shadow, di Prima.

ELIZABETH BRADFIELD

Butch Poem 6: A Countertenor Sings Handel's *Messiah*

Seven verses in, he has stepped out from the tuxed
and taffetaed quartet of soloists. He has begun to sing:
*Behold, a virgin shall conceive, and bear a son, and shall call
his son Emmanuel.* Amplified by good acoustics, the hall
is rustling accompaniment to the countertenor's solo:

Lift up thy voice with strength; lift it up, be not afraid.
Arise, shine; for thy light is come. From my seat
next to my parents, high in the mezzanine,

I can see heads turning, bending toward each other,
toward the program, small lights coming on
above the paper. My parents restrain
themselves. But the rest of the hall
is turning to the biography. Is lifting
opera glasses. Is straining ears to hear him:

Then shall the eyes of the blind be opened,
and the ears of the deaf unstopped. He is singing
the alto's part in her key, his voice light and clear.

Whispering underscores the music:
    What is this high, sweet voice in a tuxedo?
I am transfixed. I want to reach under his starched
shirtfront and find a different sex. Listen to him —

He was despised and rejected of men; a man
of sorrows, and acquainted with grief.
He's singing the score and another story alongside it:

He hid not his face from shame. Through
these old words, he is making song
of the drag queen and the bulldyke.
Let him sing without the accompaniment

of rustle. Let him sing without any doubt
between body and voice: high but not shrill,
more lovely than the wide-skirted soprano,
the chunky tenor, the dapper bass. I watch
his shine-parted hair, his weight shift at key change.

Thou art gone up on high, thou hast led captivity
captive, and received gifts for men.

Afterwards, in the bar, where anemones
splay open and salmon flick through
canals designed for our wonder, no one
mentions the countertenor. My parents,
I think, are trying to navigate the appropriate
path of the moment, as am I. But he's all
I can think of, his rolled rs, Adam's apple
lifting his tie at crescendo. Onstage,

Then shall be brought to pass the saying
that is written, Death is swallowed up in victory.

Onstage billed as high culture, this unsettlement,
this beauty applauded at last.

JERICHO BROWN

To Be Seen

You will forgive me if I carry the tone of a preacher.
Surely, you understand, a man in the midst of dying

Must have a point, which is not to say that I am dying
Exactly. My doctor tells me I might live

Longer than most, since I see him more than most.
Of course, he cannot be trusted nor can any man

Who promises you life based on his being seen.
Understand also, then, that a point and a message are

Indeed quite different. All messages issue forth from
The chosen: a lunatic, an angel, the whitest

Dove — those who hear the voice of God and other
Good music. A point, on the other hand, is made

By one who chooses but claims to have been chosen
So as not to be punished for bringing bad news:

A preacher, a poet, the doctor — those who talk
About God because they want to speak in metaphors.

My doctor, for instance, insists on the metaphor of war.
It's always the virus that attacks and the cells that fight or

Die fighting. I even remember him saying the word *siege*
When another rash returned. Here I am dying

While he makes a battle of my body — anything to be seen
When all he really means is to grab me by the chin

And, like God the Father, say through clenched teeth,
Look at me when I'm talking to you. Your healing is

Not in my hands, though I touch as if to make you whole.

Romans 12:1

I will begin with the body:
In the year of our Lord,
Porous and wet, love-wracked
And willing. In my 23rd year,
A certain obsession overtook
My body, or I should say,
I let a man touch me until I bled,
Until my blood met his hunger
And so was changed, was given
A new name
As is the practice among my people
Who are several and whole, holy
And acceptable. On the whole
Hurt by me, they will not call me
Brother. Hear me coming, and
They cross their legs. As men
Are wont to hate women,
As women are taught to hate
Themselves, they hate a woman
They smell in me, every muscle
Of her body clenched
In fits of orgasm beneath men
Heavy as heaven itself, my
Body, dear dying sacrifice, desirous
As I will be, black as I am.

NICKOLE BROWN

Etymology

God knows nothing we don't know.
We gave him every word he ever said.
 - Stephen Dunn

This is one way to trace history — a child
breathes a word into her cupped hand,
her palm trained to feel the pulse
of each consonant and vowel before she
spells into the microphone.

And this is the dictionary
she's studied: a yellowed volume,
broken spine, every word from *a*
(the Phoenician *aleph*, the Greek
alpha, the Roman A) to *zymurgy*, meaning
fermentation, dripping with wine at the end

of such a long book, such a long day, a vintage
red to be had when she's old enough to know
there is nothing she will ever memorize
that cannot be forgotten and rarely can the busy-
bee of work keep that blackbird of age
from plucking the most precious letters

from her, the siphoning of the soul
we all feel half-deflated on the couch,
glass in hand, a flashing memory of the cheering
crowd when once you got it right, how easy
to be loved when you're a child, how easy
it was to be good, everyone wants a kitten,
but a cat? Now spelling comes hard, unpracticed,

everything spellchecked
except this sentence you're composing, the one
question you want to ask, but knowing
no word ever came out of that ancient desert
changes Time, your prayer
goes something like this — *tumeric, league,*
moon-calf, pear, balm. Sea-sick sway,
orthodontics, vacuum, shunt, raven, queer,
queer, you're nothing but a queer. A hurricane,

Lord, and Sappic and bulldyke and cold cream
too. Red apron, red apple, aureole. A tangle

of sound. Oh, crowded closet, sweet mother, sweet
mother of Adam, answer me this: *why?*

REGIE CABICO

Soul Bargaining

By soul, I mean the silver that God has placed deep
inside me. Its weight runs through me, schools of dumb
fish, complicated as tiny buttons. Deeper than the front

trousers of the tricks I have rolled with. I cannot toss
myself into the East River though my soul falls from

heaven in a shower of saxophone and smoke. I am
lonelier than the iron rails of this bridge echoing the rush
of taxi cabs and a good hand job. The moon is stuck flat

to the sky. The warehouses are lit by flames of vodka.
I am bargaining my soul for grace of crows singing between

neon and this darkness. By soul, I mean in a hotel room
where a man places his lips to your ears as if they were tiny
candles, extinguishing the night with his kisses. By soul,

I mean God make me a wind instrument so I can toss myself
into the East River. The street lamps are howling for the first

slivers of light. By light, I mean falling off a bridge
wrapped in the arms of a God who knows your name.

MICHELLE CAHILL

Durga: A Self Portrait

I see an icon of myself in the dark night of a new moon.
Mothers weep for their young, married daughters, come home.
They decorate my *pandal* with sweets, *paan* and *sindoor*.

I am saving my best argument against that feminine subject,
caught in another version of the dream. Here, the heat stifles me
almost to inertia, the city shimmies with carnivalesque lights,

microphones, traffic horns, and one gaudy float after the next.
Sometimes I feel like a freak show, a cock in a frock, a new
machismo, lethal as Phoolan Devi or Buffy, the Vampire Slayer,

though my preferred epithet is Vindhayavasini. I miss a terrain
of mountains where thunder shakes, where fog is a sky snake,
where monsoon slugs engorge to the size of Krishna's penis.

Today I am androgynous, engineered as a split sex. I copy
Shiva's face, Vishnu's arms and Rama's hair. Light congeals
with strength in my bones to mend a crisis the male gods fail.

I memorize Mahisura's praise: *You are too beautiful for anything
but love,* he declares, *too delicate to fight.* Half an hour later, after
he morphs from a buffalo to an elephant, from a lion to a man,

I castrate him with a graceful blow. My suitors surrender to this
transcendental play. As for Vishnu, I spin him right round, like a record.
Men desire me for the fruit of knowledge. Want no handmaiden,

yet still a second sex, the sum of my parts being multiples of one.
My instruments, my weaponry and my props are channelled
from sensitive new age gods, with their fondness for repetition.

She whose form is sleep, hunger, shadow or thirst, I'll wear
a virgin's blush. Tomorrow I'll drink the blood of dacoits.
Send hail to the valley. Raze ten lakh's worth of rice and corn.

What I see is myself in this world: deviant, without genealogy.
Snow monkeys shiver in the deodar pines, goats loop in their shelter.
Women abandon their duties, their grief, and Vishnu is paralysed.

Sarasvati's Scribe

I came in search of other gods:
the Vedic deities, the Mahadevis.
I found only a cripple
who limps along a narrow path,
lepers with hands like turnips.
Is this the form a god takes in the global village?
These children, who have no toilet to speak of,
defecate by the sacred river,
which flows into an archipelago of weeds.
The sweet smell of latrines suffuses
every bed I sleep in.
How sunlight is a blessing.
How the smell of shampoo,
or the fading cacophony
of Israeli voices is bliss.
And if it really is Durga Puja,
where is her *wahan*?
Who would think her tiger's penis
was being used to treat impotence in China ?
Perhaps I am mistaken, today, for Lakshmi,
by the mother of a dehydrated infant
who begs a month's supply of NAN.
See — my hands have multiplied.
To germinate pink lotus flowers.
To empty out a currency in five rupee coins.
How do I explain that I am not Lakshmi,
but Sarasvati's scribe searching
for a swan's slender neck, for the right words
to convince her that breast-feeding is safer
than imported milk,
mixed with contaminated water.

Two Souls

My cat cries when I enter the garden, as
if I have aroused her from winter's dream,
or as if she wants to sing to me, her name.

What do cats dream of Lord Krishna?
A coconut shell of milk, or a glittering fish?
Now her slender limbs complete their asanas.

Now her neck arches, her jaw, an elastic.
The sharp eye constricts, discerns wind
in the quivering grass from a grass-hopper's

camouflage. But there's no mistaking *Maya*.
My cat rehearses the accurate lunge of her paw.
She cries, as one compelled; hungry, yet not.

Perhaps my being here, deserves an answer.
For weeks, I too, have watched her, how
she hunts. I've heard the moan of her catch

at dusk, which is your hour, Lord Krishna.
Then, no bird sings and only a cat with two souls
dreams of death, her stigma left on a lizard,

or on a butterfly, whatever moves towards
the shadow of meaning. As I am born of fire,
I burn, my Lord, but I sleep in your arms.

I am one Upanishad moon, on fragrant nights.
By day I am the consort of oceans, rice fields,
pale and invisible to you as the sky's temple.

RAFAEL CAMPO

Madonna and Child

By menopause, it's not just estrogen
my mother lacks. She's lost her eldest son —
that's me, the one who's queer — the doctor who
once made her very proud. These days, I do
my own wash when I'm home, I cook for her
so she can take a break from all the chores
she now refuses to assign to me.
She sits, half-watching *Oprah* through her tea's
thin steam, her squint of disapproval more
denial than it is disgust. She hears
much better than she sees — it's easier
to keep out vision than it is to clear
the air of sounds — and yet I know it's age
that stultifies her senses too. Enraged
because she's lost so much, I understand
why suddenly she looks so stunned
as from the television: " . . . Bitch, she stole
my boyfriend, my own mother did! . . . " I fold
a towel noiselessly. I know she thinks
it's garbage, sinful, crap — just as she thinks
that taking estrogen in pills is not
what God intended, no matter what
the doctors say; or that I'm gay is plain
unnatural, she can't endure such pain.
The oven timer rings. The cookies that
I've baked are done. I'll make another batch
though she won't touch them: given up for Lent.
My mother's love. I wonder where it went.

CHING-IN CHEN

Confessional: Derailment

after Ann Page's "Tips"

Flip the page back to another glass eye. Another less magical ladder. Its voice tall, slim, ready to begin.

My father emails a plea to his children situated in different cities from my grandmother's death bed. My lawyer brother later writes that I edited for grammar, he edited for sense. True, I left the pecularities in. Reading the eulogy that is not supposed to be a eulogy, my grandmother still attached to her skin. A smooth family voice narrates her life. Measuring her breaths, we are all waiting.

The artist would like to get away from observing from a distant place, putting the pieces together after everything's cooled down.

A photograph. A person within a person is all I can see. This is not one I recognize.

A sea of gold urine.

97 years, ripe and picking. Not supposed to cry, we make notes. We would all like to travel to the pure land of ultimate bliss, body disappearing with breath.

A cross evoked by the structure. Clean geometries. A monument of white legs against black. The material is mysterious.

Cannot get to the heart. What I mean to say still appearing in front of me, line by line.

Mesh against mesh.

This poem will not provide a body.

Two River Girls
a pantoum

Once there was a river glistening from your hair.
We blessed the glowing candles,
set them in the black water,
waited for a response from the gods.

We blessed the glowing candles.
I kissed your glorious mouth,
waited for a response from the gods,
hoping the beauty of our sins would be enough.

I kissed your glorious mouth,
two girls descended from salt merchants by the sea,
hoping the beauty of our sins would be enough.
We could finally travel that backwards path.

Two girls descended from salt merchants by the sea,
the water rising from what was sacred.
We could finally travel that backwards path,
the stars listening to the songs of the gods,

the water rising from what was sacred.
I am kissing a new body into flesh,
the stars listening to the songs of the gods.
There will be no mischief tonight.

I am kissing a new body into flesh.
What is beautiful can be resurrected.
There will be no mischief tonight,
only the honey between our mouths.

What is beautiful can be resurrected.
Set in the black water,
only the honey between our mouths,
where once there was a river glistening from your hair.

SEUNG-JA CHOE (최승자)(translated by Gabriel Sylvian)

I, From Early On

I was nothing from early on.
Some mold on stale bread
A stain on the wall from urine pissed time and time again
A thousand year-old corpse still coated with maggots.

No parents raised me
I slept in rat holes and fed on the livers of fleas
Blankly going to my death, anywhere would do,
I was nothing from early on.

We brush by each other
like falling comets, so
don't say that you know me.
I don't know you I don't know you
You thee thou, happiness
You, thee, thou love
That I am alive,
is just an eternal rumor.

MAYA CHOWDHRY

monsoon iii

Winter comes
my womb begins again
to prepare me for birth
to create life
a fruit for each month.
I flow
with the seasons
create my own seasons
am surprised
when the rain stops.

The soul of Kali
flying free,
Himalaya, heaven and mountain.

Before death
Kali devouring time
and after.

The one-colour-only-countries

make religious labels
to die for and red soil
is replaced with family sand.

My grandmother never knew her
mother was sikh / hindu prayers
give me my name
and leaves fall the same in
both countries.

My Lesbian Date, by Sharon Stone

I have stones in my pockets
so I may drown
  as
the sea eats my ankles
I hear the cry of my sister
stoned under Islam
for taking a woman
to her naked breast
  my instinct tells me
that bisexual women
are afraid of the taste
  you tell me my kisses
are sweet
but there's the sour
hunger of women
who take marriage vows
to avoid
the stones
thrown

JAMES CIHLAR

Twin Cities

This city park sign tells me
Land that once was the highest point
Is now the lowest,

Just as where there once were trees
There now are lakes,
And in a corresponding spot across the river,

Where there once were lakes,
There now are trees.
Curtainless windows at night

Show the clear-cut inscapes
Of once old buildings,
Now white angles and recessed lighting.

On the freeway I passed an old-fashioned RV,
The kind I wished for when I was young
So my family would be safe

Even on yellow-lit highways, with
The impersonal landscape fading
Into oily black mist.

In a trailer like that,
Parked in his mistress's driveway,
My father locked us one night

So that they could fuck in privacy
Inside her ranch-style house.
When I woke up, my mother

Had the county and her lawyer
Unlocking the door.
So why should I daydream now

About a life on the road?
Last week a solicitor rang the doorbell
Of the home I live in with my husband,

And I looked out the window
Instead of answering.
I saw from the back

An old man in a trench coat and hat
Who could have been my father.
He left a pamphlet damning homosexuals,

Which fell from the lintel
When I opened the door.
How can we live like this?

Maybe by knowing
I live in a city that is one half
Of a whole,

And by knowing the rule here is change —
Where something is removed,
It must also be returned,

Just as I know, with time,
Where I have once been empty
I will someday be full,

And in the places
where I once have received,
I may later give.

ANDREA COHEN

Rolling and Walking

Let's be clear: some
of the walking wounded
are confined to chairs.
Their hairdos, like
the past and future,
are elements somewhat
beyond their control.
One woman shows
how the chair
goes forward and back
by virtue of her breath,
directed. She says:
they don't call it
the suck and blow
chair because that sounds
pornographic. She sucks
and blows, turns three
tight circles, and out
of breath, laughs:
those are my moves.
Her moves are in
her head too, where
she dreams she's walking,
pursuing her chair.
She was asleep
when the accident happened.
She remembers a man
reaching in through the pick-up's
smashed back window to hold
her head in place. It was
her neck that had broken.
But her head was clear, she
was awake, she closed
her eyes to keep dust out.
There was a lot
of dust. Some was settling.
Some people in another
vehicle were already dust
or about to become it.
She could hear sirens, which
she took as a good sign:

help was near and she could hear.
A siren on an otherwise
bright day when your boyfriend falls
asleep can mean disaster or all clear.
It matters if he's at the wheel
of a truck, or turning over after love.
Sometimes we hear glass
breaking, sometimes our own
bones. Sometimes you can't know
what you hear or don't,
what ringing's real or in your head.
She tells of going to Sea World
now, how it's different: *I still love*
the seals and whales, she says, *but I*
don't get tired. At the end of the day,
people on their feet, they feel
fatigue. I forget about their troubles.
Studies of lottery winners suggest
people are roughly as happy
before as they are after.
She said to her parents
in intensive care: *Aren't we lucky*
to meet so many nice folks?
We're walking or rolling
through Sea World, through stop
signs, through the Valley of Death.
We can suck and blow.
We keep going.
That's all I know.

Self Portrait with the Cinnabons

The Cinnabon Indians prefer
to be addressed as the Cinnabon
Native Americans. Any fool knows this.
What's that? Oh, mille apologia.
I misheard. It's the Assiniboine tribe
of Montana, not at all related
to the Cinnabon peoples who sell us
sticky buns we love in airports, those
fat laden frosted squares
we wouldn't touch elsewhere.
But the limbo of airports permits
such reckless decadence. Dough
treats seem tame compared with the dangers
of lift-off and landing, so we allow
ourselves the sugar coma,
the rush associated with high-
risk ventures such as love
or lust, which are never far
from any terminal. If you're old enough,
you'll remember walking your beloved
to the gate, across the tarmac, even on to the plane.
Back then, you could step from Cincinnati
into the waiting room at O'Hare and never know
who might greet you. This was before the rise
of the Cinnabon people, who thrive
on our appetites for yeasty sweets, which
may have increased with tighter security measures.
The Assiniboine remember when everything
changed, how that happened slowly and all
of a sudden, and then from the spirit
of the U.S. government came Schlitz
in crushable cans and trailers
and the rez, where not much changed.
If you were a plains Indian
in Montana, you could lose everything,
you could lose your shirt, but
you'd still have your hair, and if
you're Assiniboine and you tell anybody,
hey man, you're beautiful, you mean
his hair, her hair. If you get
very close to someone, if
he trusts you, he'll let you
brush his hair, which he never
cuts, outside the trailer, or inside of it.
And if you're Assiniboine or Gros Ventre

or anybody else for that matter,
you'll have to put your hair in netting
if you work in the Cinnabon.
It's the law and it's hygienic.
And if you're Assiniboine, there's
another advantage, since they believe
that if you haven't lead a righteous life,
when you die, you have to gather
all the hair you ever lost
on earth and burn it.
That's a real limbo for you,
a bonafide purgatory. I saved
a plastic sack of my own hair
clippings for no good reason
and peek in at the chestnut
and graying locks. They resemble
a delicate invertebrate which the remorseful
fingers of all my ex-loves
might like to pet. The sack of hair
is like a creature who used
to travel the world, downing
Cinnabons as if there were
no Cincinnati, no tomorrow, but who
no longer gets out much. If I
get my DNA tested, I may find
links to the Cinnabons or the Assiniboines,
but in the end, identity is a matter
of splitting hairs, isn't it?
It all comes down to having
someone you trust enough to comb
your infinite tresses or shine your bald pate.
When you get to the pearly gates
or whatever version of that
your faith allows, there may
or may not be a Cinnabon stand there.
They may or may not offer you a job
as a management trainee. If they do,
take it. Everything in life
and death is temporary: beauty,
the icing on the cake, the voice
over the loud speaker that says
the ground time, while brief, allows
for a swift dash to the Cinnabon stand,
which for a limited time only,
in lieu of cash will take as payment
the wisdom of the Assiniboines
and one nomadic lock of hair.

STEVEN CORDOVA

**Eating Fallen Fruit is More Humane
Than Plucking an Apple from a Tree**

At the fallen fruit produce section of the trendy corporate
chain, Fallen Fruit, you may purchase a wide variety of
fallen fruits. You may select said fallen fruit yourself
or you may purchase the far more convenient, if less
environmentally sound, pre-packaged fallen fruit.
Whichever you decide to do, be wise, remember: outside,
it may be warm, there may be a breeze, but transporting
your fallen fruit home, high on the fact that you are walking
instead of emitting harmful gases into the air (unless,
of course, you are), take care not to swing your "green"
reusable bag like the fallen fig (fag) you are. For there are
all kinds of fallen fruit out there, many of them rotten to the
core, and they terrorize the Big Apple, beating up on other
fallen fruit so they don't have to feel like such fallen fruit
themselves. Once home, your precious fallen fruit safe and
not any more bruised than it needs to be, you may bake a
fallen fruit apple pie and you may even go so far as cutting
and serving this conscientiousness little treat at a fallen
fruit party where your socially conscious guests, all of them
dressed in imitation leather, will say that though you're
quite the handsome devil, and a fallen fruit through and
through, you at least have come along. You are "aware"
and you would never pluck an apple from a tree.

EDWARD DEBONIS

Sacred Heart

In 1961, I'm a fourth grade altar boy at
Sacred Heart Church, scared about fucking
up the Latin Mass. During Lent we kneel in
veneration of the Host, which is encased in
a gold monstrance.

When you pass it you must genuflect on two
knees because you can't get any closer to God
than this. I wait until I am the only altar boy
there keeping guard. I unbutton the front of my
cassock, unzip my pants and show God my

grade school cock. I hate God for making me
sick. I knew in sixth or seventh grade that I was a
homo. In ninth grade, I stood in the back of the
church until Communion, then went with my friends
to smoke cigarettes and play poker. After high school
I stayed out of Sacred Heart Church for thirty years.

For their fiftieth anniversary my parents renewed their
wedding vows at Sacred Heart. Before the Mass, my
boyfriend Vinnie and I meet Father Vaughn who hugs
me. Such a long time. He needs Eucharistic ministers.
Vinnie and I look at each other. We know this ride

is out of our control. At Communion, we walk to the
center of the altar and bow, just like we do on Sunday's
at Dignity New York, our queer Catholic Church. We are
the first to receive the bread and wine with Father Vaughn.
We stand on either side of him with two chalices of the

Blood of Christ. Father Vaughn descends the stairs to my
parents who receive the host. Vinnie and I follow. Vinnie
gives the wine to my Mom, I to my Dad. They smile at us
and we return to the altar where the community comes to partake.
I am holding on as my life comes up to the altar one by one,

lie after lie, shame after shame, aunts and uncles, cousins, friends
of my parents, parents of my friends. I have not seen their faces
grow whiter, their eyes glassier and smaller, the skin around
them being pinched by fingers of time. Some I thought were dead,
but there they are. Ghosts, smiling at me, coming toward

me, hands folded carrying the body of Christ in their
mouths, standing before me I see them through the blur
of tears, my voice barely able to say "the Blood of Christ."
When I met Vinnie, I followed his coal eyes and satin
skin to Dignity. Queer Proud Catholics. He led me

back. He showed me his soul and then I found my own.
He has the same faith of those marching up the aisles at
Sacred Heart last weekend. They honestly believe, yet
still weep at the dying of each other. Vinnie is my past,
out in the open. No longer hiding or ashamed, we are put
on the altar together because of Mom and Dad and God.

NEIL DE LA FLOR

Their Fathers

Permit our fathers permission to kiss.
We are permitted the use of our host

hands like Baptists. We are Buddhists now. We
are pigments the ancient scriptures don't men-

tion in myths. The nun who likes us likes foot-
ball. We can see it in her eyes, the way

she winks at guests like a pervert as they
walk down the aisle. Death & Company

rings our fathers. *Amen* and pop the cork.
They kiss, of course, deep, as if no one else

is around to bear witness to this. Our
fathers dry their eyes. This is paradise

in an unclean city. The flowers wear
yellow tuxedos. We are silent in

black celebration, the awful scars of
our fathers turn to face the emerging

stars, the new dimension of Daddies. The
woman wearing the stupid, yellow dress

with the bullhorn swears at us in the an-
cient language of hairdo. The nun swears back.

JOSEPH DELGADO

cure for bad dreams

she slices cucumber
into a bowl of hot water
leaves it on the window sill
says it for san isidro

when he comes to swallow
her children
when he comes to scratch away
the skin, cleanser smell,

the creases of her thighs.
fat, she ambles to the bathroom
light like a moth,
to feel her finger

where her man slapped
a tooth from its jaw
its resting place.
she comes to the

couch side, rubs hot oil
on my head, the underside of
my chin.
says the angels will lick

at it, come like starved dogs
to a bowl of sour milk.
come to restitch the busted
nose, chin, clean my tongue.

she wraps herself in her
polyester nightgown, robe of tattered ends.
moves through the house
like a morning shadow.

dipping her finger
into the water bowl, to make
sure its cool enough,
make sure this santo of quiet nights,

comes to keep the bad dreams
away, keep them rotted on the sill
like the night moth
scraping its tongue against the window.

CHERYL DUMESNIL

Chosen

Dust and brown leaves blowing across
the soccer field, a traffic light
bouncing on its pole, the gusting wind
suddenly cool, I roll up the window,
slam the car into park, run up the driveway,
yanking quilts off the clothesline.
I had seen it coming — smoky clouds
billowing over the hill, crawling our way.
The screen door slaps in its frame,
and I find her curled on the bed, waiting.
When she was six years old they told her
the world would end like this —
a muscled beast filling her sky, thunder
rattling glass panes. Her father
hoarded blankets, stashed bottled water,
canned beans under his bed. He packed
a St. Christopher medal in her lunch box,
hung the worn thread of a scapular
around her neck as she left for school.
He told her: *When it happens, He will*
appear as a bright light, turn away
from windows, only the chosen will be
saved. I drop the quilts on the floor
and lie down beside her, sweep
hair from her collar, kiss her damp neck.
A thunder blast. The first white bolt.
I slide my hands inside her shirt
and hold her. Yes, chosen. Yes, saved.

BLAS FALCONER

Never

> *But Peter declared, "I will never leave you."*

I see that far: next week in empty pockets,
next month in coins scattered on a bed
beside a ring. Once, I fell and hit
my head. I opened my eyes and couldn't see.
Then, I could. Not before my mother sang
softly in my ear, *Okay, okay*, but she
wasn't sure. She squeezed my hand in her hands.
How much the gesture wants to say — .

This is how it will happen: one voice
over many. The constellations shifting above.
Nothing else will matter. Not the men.
What they say or what you say.
It won't count. It won't mean a goddamn thing.
You'll save yourself. Understand? Yourself.

DANIELLE MORGAN FERIS

Passover

for Vered & Ari Lev in 2006

If she wants to she eats bread today
If she wants to she doesn't eat bread
today. But today the name she
was named to love Israel
in cannot love the taste
of clean cupboards nor
the land that lives by the clock
of Jewish words. The one
that shuts down on Friday
night and rests until Saturday.
It tells her when to make
borscht and never runs out of
farfel at the supermarket.
The buses shut down and
only men can initiate
divorce because that's what
the men decided. Her
name is Rose.

She cannot
love the wall that lets this
clock run. That lets
a Settler shoot into trees,
watch someone fall
to the ground. And leave
without repercussions. She can't
love the clock
that takes a Palestinian's time
to wait on thirty different lines
to maybe send this person who
shot his uncle to jail maybe.

She bought olive oil stronger
than all others
in old soda bottles
label ripped off
but cannot love the walk
she took
home to make dinner

to celebrate freedom
when she looks in young male eyes
who cannot love anymore
checking IDs, yelling in the face of
her friend Palestinian
blue Palestinian green
American Secular Israeli Queer
and together,
she resists

the clock
wound by black coated prayer,
with pieces made by red, white,
and blue suited prayer
by no prayer she knows

The clock that hides
women beaten by their husbands or
cleaning houses far away from home.
The clock that closes
restaurants and roads, so
she can't eat where and when she wants to
on the one brief day
Israeli workers get to rest
and she can't march with Pride
while children wait detained
next to tanks that bear the star
she wears with six points.

She can't ever go home
without their smiles
at the soldiers, their return
to half walls of cement
posters pasted up.

If she wants to she cannot
love the way she wants to.

Though she can move back
to a land whose clock
does not remember
her. Does not always
save a box of *farfel*
for her breakfast
or rest enough for her
to rest too.

Back to rapid time and people blind
fixed on sermons at the temple
where she feels at home.

Silent at the *Seder*
she misses land
she cannot love,
curses her mother's tradition,
defies her father's hate,
won't eat bread today cannot
love today
the way she wants to.

JOHN FRAZIER

The Wax Museum

It's not your fault. How easy the tremolo could flow from any
silky Motown crooner, but they are your words in your mouth. It's a new year
pushing you into mid-life. The dog, still exuberantly chasing sea foam, bounces
amongst dead things that have come in with the tide. You mean to write about god
and celestial beings, but all you conjure is a father who on Sundays
would drive out to the ocean taking turns with each of you in the breakers until salt
crusted your faces. You are older now than he was then. The air is crisp.
Later you will wait in a waiting room as a friend's blood is drawn;
the dark rows of matter could be yours or anyone's. The wax
museum was a show that played Sunday evenings, cranked in on a farmhouse
transistor. You'd listen for hours to songs of heartbreak and regret fighting
phantoms as the sun disappeared. You might still find some remnants
of the day — salt on your cheek or the body swaying, as is its custom, remembering
the push then pull of the ocean before it gives way to some dreaming.

J. NEIL C. GARCIA

Melu

Why must it be strange
that a world should spring
from an itch?
Melu, creator of the Bilaan,
was as black as a stone's pure heart.
In the first twilight he rose,
his eyes and teeth glinting like stars
in the horizonless sky.
Sensing a gap all over his body,
he discovered
he desired nothing
but to rub himself with his hands.
Palm against skin he scratched
and stroked, and flake
by sheer flake the earth drifted away
from his shape,
to gather in a heap below him.
As he rubbed, and his rubbings fell,
he felt himself grow lighter
and whiter.
Soon he was invisible as air,
floating above the crumbled shell
of his old self.
This story tells us:
creation is the body
shorn clean
off a god's brilliant need
for formlessness.
We cannot help but wonder:
as our skins slip past each other
in this life,
do we not help
this first sacrifice to proceed –
its work a sacred duty
meant for us all along?
Out of love, or pain,
and every time our edges touch,
we grind our itchy bodies
hard against this world's darkness –
praying we, too, may know light.

XL

What happens to me after
is not anything I can predict:
as we are sometimes told,
from an ending just might gesture
a beginning. I would like to believe, as did
my people whose breath was soil —
I shall remain useful
even if only as an aspect of soil.
Out of my feet sweet yams perhaps, my fingers
curled forth into the graceful backs of snails,
from my stomach something flesh-bound or fat
like pulpy shoot or vine with off-white blooms
dangling from its sides, my tongue,
that difficult slab of weathered wood,
just might whisper its new-found language
in fragrant syllables of herb and mushroom
and amber sap. Consider it:
anything is possible
when you are one with earth —
giving ground in which dreams stab downward,
take root like love, and come to fruit.

Weight

The soul travels light, so we've heard:
it carries nothing into this world,

nothing out of it. And yet, tonight,
over good buttered bread, by contraries

we're told a different prospect:
the things we give away, we share

or lose in offering, only those can we,
past the dark and icy passage, bring.

This gentle teller's no mere stranger,
not to us, nor this hard-won truth:

his certain hand that scrawled its script
inside our heads, above faith's white table

these twenty years has raised the body up,
with a splash of water has washed it new,

rubbed its fevered brow and lips with oil,
to nudge it softly back to the waiting soil

as he sends its restless tenant on his way.
Having ably ministered to flesh and spirit,

he knows, we know, whereof he speaks.
And so, we think ahead to our own crossing

over, how cumbrous must our baggage be:
the salt-edged laughter, the late and early loves

given fully to others and not returned,
the air begrudged us by a tightfisted life,

the peace of mind, the dreams forgone
and all because of who and *what* we were —

crammed all into desire's many bulging sacks
that ground us forever in our heaven's earth.

RJ GIBSON

Agnosticism

Maybe there is a Heaven,
& maybe
there's someone in it.
Maybe
you'll stare at the caramelized bread
of your grilled cheese sandwich & see
the face of your salvation.
Maybe you'll say
Oh, God
at almost the right time:
your car will be t-boned
but your niece won't break her neck.
Maybe they'll use the jaws of life,
extract you
from the car, get you to the OR on time,
but on the table you die,
for a minute,
go into that great white light
rippling with lilac about the edges,
before you're pulled back
into your life
where the only thing shining
is a bank of incandescent bulbs.

Meditations on Mortality

These are the ways I wish not to die:

Cancer of the anything, heart attack, lightning strike, fire, drowning,
asphyxiation, shark or stingray. Collapsing building, plane crash, sniper, drive-
by, mugging, AIDS or any sort of flu. I don't want to be smeared beneath the
Rhino Propane Refill truck as I'm crossing the Lowe's parking lot, two cheap
toilet seats beneath each arm. Not on a sofa with the last four or five

people in the world who love me, gathered while I expire. Not in a hospital bed,
demented from drugs and fatty embolisms, begging for water and someone to
keep that *man* from the window. Not from the stings of an agitated hive of
Africanized bees, rattlesnake bite, any Snake bite. Not from SARS or tissue necrosis.
Not from nicotine poisoning because I lost my head and frolicked,
rolled in a field of high tobacco Somewhere in the South. Not in the middle of
fucking — normal

fucking or the sort of sexual misadventure that ends with some poor maid
finding a washed-up celebrity hanging in his hotel room, stiff as a board. Pit
Bull attack, Mastiff attack, attack by any sort of dog that's been the minion of Satan
in any drive-in movie. Not Elvis, Marilyn, Jayne, John, Jimi, or Mama
Cass. Not Ronald Reagan. I don't want the luxury of forgetting even the smallest
evils I have done.

Not alone, not crowded either.
When I die: give my books to a library;

Toss my underwear and socks in the garbage —
I don't want someone else trying to fill what I've stretched out.

Give away my clothes and shoes,
Especially the Kenneth Coles and DKNY; drink my liquor.

Drag my mattress, my linens, my pillows to the field:
burn them in the middle of the night.

Let that fire light, that heat rise,
let that smoke be a black spire:

a subtly different black, a Mars black,
lapping against the black night sky.

Let that blaze disturb someone elses's night,
let the fear of spreading flames keep him from sleep,

keep me in his mind.

What We Call the World is Always the Immediate

Today every window, every curtain
you can stand to have open
is open
and it is humid, so humid, the air
so close
everything feels suspended,
as though it all hangs
from gossamer chains –
like something from *Gawain*
or JK Rowling. Suspended,
about to tip.
Something is about to happen.
Every hair
that is your hair
aprickle. Something
is about to spill.
You want outside,
you want change, want other,
want for the simple sake of it.

Facebook keeps saying: Connect
with John. Send him a message, Write
on his Wall. But John
is dead. You learned that weeks ago;
on Facebook, of course.
Maybe this is the Afterlife
2.0 – where we're all just electrons,
bits and bytes uploaded,
never aging in that perpetual ether.
But here, on Earth,
there'll just be rain.
It will come in the dark,

so you don't have to see it.
You want the earth soaked,
softened 'til you might spoon it up
and redistribute. You want water
to soak in. You want the world
soft as a body. You're always waiting
for the softness of bodies. You want water
to soak in deep. The way stress
and sorrow do. Resting deep
until it surfaces like a spring,
or spasms deep beneath

your shoulder, or sobs as you brush your teeth.

There's no idea how long John lay dead,
alone in his apartment, before he was found.
And of course the self-indulgent pity party
that that could be *your* future. Oh, underloved,
oh, needy. Your best friend asks how you can stand
to stay in this shitty shitty town, what
there is that keeps you. Abundance,
you say, so much:

the hills of course, the maples of course,
the tulip poplars, the locusts
thorny as Sunday dinners: the ragweed of course,
the multiflora rose,
the ironweed, its shaggy violet florets blunt
as punks: of course the poppy, the bleeding
heart, the milkweed of course, its pom pon blooms pink
and common as candy,
its pods like a crocodile's brows:
the ragweed, the lungwort:
of course the fancy columbines
each creamy heart
like a fighting cock's top knot:

of course the yellowjacket sudden and startling
as caution signs, detours in an unknown city:
the bumblebee clumsy, hungry for sweet,
the bald-faced hornet hungry for anything:

the sowbug the slug, the lunescent grub
bright as developing thoughts:
of course the black beetle, the basil, oregano,
the heirloom tomatoes: of course the drizzle, the deluge, the shower:
the moon fickle as a celebutante
with her shifting face: the snow of course:
the stratus, the cirrus, the cumulonimbus: of course dawn
and night, of course the earth
so ready to burst
that it smells as if everything is about to happen
only some of it good.

BRENT GOODMAN

Everyone Wonders

Told Hell awaited me by 6th grade.
Best friend. More for being a Jew than

wearing my glasses in the showers.
My parents didn't suspect he was

black. So polite on the phone, Dan Rhone.
There's something I didn't believe in

and it was all my fault. There's something
he believed in and he was all wrong.

I've never wished ill upon a soul.
To be chosen: Everyone wonders.

BENJAMIN S. GROSSBERG

Beetle Orgy

Bloom up from the earth, blooming and curling
like ribbon, and at semi-regular intervals
sprouting leaves: almost the border art
of a Celtic manuscript, the vines up along the fence
of this old tennis court. Amid the wreck

of the net, the cracks of the surface, the rust
along the poles still standing, the vines
are a saving delicacy. Not jarring at all,
though incongruous — except as a reminder
that the school yard will gladly take this place

back in a few untended years, that between
the vines and grass, the tennis courts
will be ground into meal and digested.
I stop at one of the vine edgings caught
by even finer detail: the leaves themselves

are digested; they have been eaten to
irregular lace, and the perpetrators are still here —
five of them across one particular leaf, lined up
straight and even, like cars in a parking lot.
Beetles: their backs a lustrous green and copper,

taken from the kiln hot, thrown on a bed of saw dust
that burst into flame, then lidded over
so the vacuum could draw the metal oxides
to the surface. At first it looks like there are five,
but now I see that there are seven, no eight —

and that in three of the spaces, beetles
are doubled up, one mounting, back legs
twitching as if running and getting nowhere;
and one mounted, also moving, slightly rocking
in back, close to the point of intersection —

or penetration — in any case, where the bodies
touch. And here I come to it — amid the advancing
vines and decrepit court: they're on other leaves, too,
all around — coupling in company, hundreds of them,
the rows melding to make a single metallic band.

Back in Houston, a friend had parties —
lawn bags in the living room numbered with tape
to store guest clothing; plastic drop cloths
spread out in the spare bedroom (cleared of furniture
for the occasion), a tray of lubricants, different

brands in tubes or bottles, labels black, red, and silver
— a high tea sensibility. The artifacts remained
uncollected in his apartment for days, even
weeks after, when I would drop by to find his talk
transformed, suddenly transcendental —

the communality, he told me, the freedom: not
just from the condom code (HIV negative I
was never invited) but freed of individuation —
nothing less than rapture, men more than brothers,
a generosity of giving and taking, to both give

and take greedily, that he had experienced
nowhere else. Could I understand that?
The room pulsing as if inhabited by
a single animal, caught up in a single sensibility.
Could I understand? I could read transformation

in his face, could see his eyes, feel him trying
to tell me something: to offer this reliable revelation —
what he always knew would come, but what always
in coming disarmed him. As he talked I looked around
the spare bedroom, attempting to see it

in terms other than lust — a couple of dozen men,
how they would have lined up, become a single
working unit on clear plastic, how their bodies
might have formed a neat chain. I looked around
and tried; couldn't I understand that?

So each beetle a tiny scarab, a dime-size jewel
that glints in the sun. I lean over and touch
their backs with the tip of my finger: running
up and down the bright, smooth surface
like piano keys, hard enough to feel resistance

but not to interject foreign music. Together they form
a band of light, a band of glaze, the gold leafing
that shadows the vines in Celtic manuscripts, a living art.
Maybe that's how it was at my friend's parties —
God leaning over the house on a casual tour

of the wreck of the world, noticing ornamentation
where it wasn't expected. Moved to add
His touch, He reaches a hand through the clouds, runs
His finger over the hard arch of their backs, covering
the length of each spine with the tip;

each man brightens at the touch, comes to know
something expected, unexpected, and tenuous —
and God, also, comes to some knowledge
as if for the first time, is distracted and pleased
by the collective brightness of human skin. . . .

Then I think of God fitting the roof back on
my friend's house, and exhaling, satisfied —
just like me as I walk away
from the tennis court, just like the men inside.

JEREMY HALINEN

Some Nights Even God Is Agnostic

I found it in an empty box of toys.
What I mean is: when I emptied
the box of its toys, I found it
in its emptiness. I know no other way
to say this, so I'm waiting for the world
to make me new, suitable words.
Just as some songs are desperate to be sung,
so are some words to be spoken,
to transcend the universe of not.
An emptiness in my mind tonight
threatens to swallow the sky.
But the stars stay where they are.

Stranger

When I don the body
of the serpent, I see,
   for the first time,
the dawn and realize
   what a yawn it is
to be me: I am that I am —
   so what? To have every
perspective at once:
   as good as having
none. Goddamn this
   woman, this man
who see these trees
   from solid land alone.
I'll show them. Hey lady, taste
   the fruit of this tree.
You'll see, you'll see.

ROBERT HAMBERGER

The Shellfish Eater

> And all that have not fins and scales in the seas, and in the rivers, of
> all that moves in the waters, and of any living thing which is in the
> waters, they shall be an abomination unto you:
>   - Leviticus 11:10

Am I salt in God's eye
for loving what feeds me?

Thou shalt not is a shark
nosing through waters, scenting blood.

When I bless every oyster and mussel
my throat knows abomination.

I could swallow the ocean
cool my tongue on wet flesh.

This slippery taste
a birthmark etched by God.

The Hug

Christians sing in the market, praise the Lord,
crowding the pavement with their happiness:
all those grins stinging the air while they bless
his name. I cut through them like a sword
of righteousness, as if your word
still sings inside my mouth, as if I miss
your rage hand in hand with your gentleness.
If you were here we could do what we did
years ago when we stood in the middle
of singing Christians and hugged each other
like proud queens. You kissed me in their huddle,
resting your head briefly on my shoulder,
parting their waves with a simple cuddle.
Hold me now. I can't hear you. Sing louder.

FORREST HAMER

Goldsboro narrative #24:
Second benediction

for Mr. Holman

Knowing we still needed to dance,
the man who kept company with men

played the church organ sassy

and let us sway ourselves near him
even as we gathered still beside him,

watching his thin fingers talk the way they dared

when the sermon had been made
and we lingered to pray for sound

because the body waits for sound. We waited

for the moment his fingers spoke in their tongues,
listened for the urgent translation into this:

We have returned to a blessed place;
Our family is here with us, even the dead and not-born;
We are journeying to the source of all wonder,

We journey by dance. Amen.

Slave song

for Sterling Brown

Don't want to be singin no slave songs.
Slavery is over, and I don't want to hear em.
I don't care about rememberin old things.
Don't be bringin no slave songs.

Slavery is over, and I don't want to hear em.
My feets can move just as free as they please.
Don't be bringin no slave songs.
Don't be askin bout no slave shuffle.

My feets can move just as free as they please.
I got no need to stay in one place.
Don't be askin bout no slave shuffle.
A body cain't barely feel itself that way.

I got no need to stay in one place.
Don't go speakin to me bout no religion.
A body cain't barely feel itself that way.
God ain't done nothin but look at me and grin.

Don't go speakin to me bout no religion.
My old master think hisself God's onliest son.
God ain't done nothin but look at me and grin.
Freedom ain't come from none of these ways.

My old master think hisself God's onliest son.
I don't care about rememberin old things.
Freedom ain't come from none of these ways.
Don't want to be singin no slave songs.

Below and beside

My friends were talking about how a vertical view
of divinity presumes God is above us and male,
the way in families fathers may be head.
They wondered about a lateral sense of things,
God among us on earth, between and therefore within us.

I was listening and I wasn't, thinking at once
about the place of the unconscious to the conscious
— below, presumably, but possibly beside:
a shape in the dark is both a toy chest and a coffin,
someone else a friend as well as a parent

as well as self. I have known for some time
how much there is I do not want to see —
pockets of air where matters wait for me
to notice. Once, while I was visiting back East,
a white woman hanged herself from the invisible.

No one else paid attention, so I saw her
and I didn't. It was the last night's dream,
dreams staying themselves beside what else there is.
Something the matter in my life was beginning to place
itself, the woman not the stranger I could claim.

Probably, my friends were just revisioning
the claim to gods: that God hangs alongside
awful between us, no longer dominating.

REGINALD HARRIS

Sunday Self-Portrait

First Gospel then Ravel.
The body slow, tired out from
dancing, making love
the night before. Scrambled eggs and sausage
   take my hand
for late breakfast, then wake him,
staying hands that long to roam,
   La Mer
rediscover rich furred skin
beneath its fingers.

Back from travels —
   not a playa I just crush a lot
work drop-off, gym, infirm parents —
return to drift while reading poetry,
   can't stop praising His name, I
an Ellington soundtrack,
maybe Mingus, Barber, Glass,
between contented purrs of
   In-di-go
neighbor's cat,
   needle on the record put the needle on the record
upstairs
in search of milk, slow mice

to dream of words slow dancing,
   Do nothing till you hear
hands trailing across the body,
   waters gently shirred
silk-thin breezes
   that thing, that thing, that thing
a kiss that echoes, moans, raises
   rocking gently
      and talking gently
the memory of choirs,
   In my house
flashing lights, hard beats
   no one
heartbeats
   ever thanked him
his musk,

Goin' up yonder
the body's music
                Goin' up yonder
praisesongs
                        Goin' up yonder   to be with my Lord
        from a muted radio.

JEN HOFER

Resolved

It is impossible to describe, thus no description will occur, no description will accumulate, no description or dissection will accrue or clump or clot or refuse to clot so as to call to mind a black plague sewer or the speed, relatively speaking, with which a river might whisk away   the dead or their extra limbs.

*

Resolved

Enduring: like succulents, only more difficult propagation, like street dogs, only no scraps, like hydroelectric dams, only no water, no stars, no sense of spin unless you count this dizzying administrative stasis,   this formulaic mouthing of vocabulary in the shape of sentences.

FANNY HOWE

The Apophatic Path

1

What isn't what is

not Discover me!
Or Try to find me.

If being is finding,

can you find me?
Who to, this address?

. . .

Being as close to a shadow
as a color

what isn't
is what is

and I can't see
but know as no.

Non amari sed amare.

. . .

Or will a question be,

"Is the discovery for real me?"

Signature a stone???

Like what isn't
is what is

when not being
ever ever ever found!

2

Basic science

will blend ghostness
among enemies.

Now bodies cemented

down in monster denominations
to be counted

one of the walking
corpses I see whitening

and emptying
under a sun

makes me know me
to be no one.

3

Walk to developmental old trombone — I —

seeking to be found —
inside time! — by one whose blues

seek by speaking tunes to
this specific city afternoon

of bread, fumes, and orange
nasturtiums — am, still, solo —

even the base of me being, unknown.

AZWAN ISMAIL (translated by Shahril Nizam)

Lamentation of Lust

Torrid Tuesday evening,
ignites my thirst
for antiquated ballads,
ancient legends
and jubilant cheers of revolutionists.

But you have not yet
come to witness me
sing a lengthy libretto;
a deviant opera (they
named it so).
I am still waiting for you.

When night arrives,
I long for
the full moon,
the perfect rainbow and
the arrival of mysterious shadows
with angelic wings.

An exquisite whip
has been placed
on the coffee table
for you to strike
me with repeatedly
until dawn:
o unbending poet.

We will then undress
each other and spread
ourselves on solid ground;
bound together by our fervent embrace
until the cold floor beneath us
absorbs the warmth from our bodies;
its heat then rising to the heavens above,
arousing the angels
and their guests
who grow envious of
all the ardent sinners on earth.

Keluhan Ghairah

panas petang selasa
membuatkan aku dahaga
pada syair-syair lama,
cerita-cerita dongeng dulukala
& segala sorak-sorai para
revolusiner.

tapi kau belum jua
datang menyaksikan aku
menyanyikan libreto panjang
sebuah opera sesat (mereka
menggelarkannya sebegitu).
aku tetap menunggumu.

menjelang malam
aku merindui
bulan terang,
pelangi sempurna &
bayang-bayang misteri
bersayap malaikat.

ada cemeti mahal
sudah aku letak
atas meja kopi
untuk nanti kau libas
aku sehingga subuh:
sang penyair
masih berdegil.

kemudian kita
akan telanjang bersama
atas lantai keras
berpelukan mesra
sehingga lantai sejuk
menjadi hangat,
habanya mengalir ke
syurga atas sana
hinggakan bidadari &
pelanggannya
terangsang, serta-merta
cemburu pada para pendosa.

We will not
drown ourselves in guilt,
for our heavenly reward
is not yet ours,
nor do we need it.
It is merely a worn-out fantasy
created by Man.

(Reality is infinitely perfect
but we are blind,
for we give value
to things that
are not ours.)

kita tidak akan
rasa bersalah
kerana pahala
belum kita punya,
kita juga tidak
memerlukannya. ia
cuma fantasi lama
ciptaan manusia.

(realiti serba sempurna
tapi kita buta
kerana suka meletakkan
harga pada sesuatu
yang bukan milik kita.)

MARIA JASTRZĘBSKA

Planting Out Cabbages

I envied the altar boys
their white cassocks
and being allowed to ring the bell
before communion, but I had my eye
on the priest's job.

Folded tea towels over my arm
and picking up a plastic doily mat,
trance-like round the kitchen, I copied
the solemn way he walked
carrying a silver tray
of flesh and blood which had come to us
from Mary's womb
in the unlikely form of fruit.

Years later, the tai chi teacher traced
the shape of clouds through the air,
turning in slow motion on the spot.
She spoke of moving meditation.
I knew exactly what she meant.
I'd had years of sermons
when the priest thundered about the evil of divorce.
But then there was one (there's always one
and for that I do thank God)
a priest who said prayer was something
you could do anywhere —
devotion found in the simplest task
even planting out cabbages,
which the brothers did in the vegetable patch
behind the chapel.

Tonight I wash my hands and face
at the sink, warm water slipping on my skin.
Delicious task.
We've come in from a chill, starry night
after seeing friends. You're falling asleep on the sofa —
a defiant look on your face — and won't go to bed
just like your daughter
when she's too tired to know it.
The house is quiet and it's late;
every part of the silver darkness
is there outside. I pull the curtains across.

Seeing the Pope on TV

The figure of an old man
In flowing robes
Sunlight pouring on his head
Shining on his kindly face
His outstretched arms.

Not only that
But what it meant
When they elected a Pole — our Karolek
Chosen by the cardinals.
'Did you see the news
A Pole on TV?'

He could have been
An uncle or a grandfather
When he spoke in English,
I know the accent by heart
Recognised it straightaway
The roll of the r's in corruption.
He'd blessed the babies and the newlyweds,
He was talking about the evil
Which threatens decent family life
I didn't smile
I knew it was me
He was talking about.

JOE JIMÉNEZ

Thirsting

When you read this poem, you will, at times, call out his name.
Unthinkingly. It is your costumbre, after all, to love like this.
When you read this poem, the bed on which you sleep is not empty. Isn't
cold. Ain't dead. Ain't suficiente, still.

When you read this poem, the lights outside leak orange glaringly, and
you are not preparing his favorite meal, because that meal can't be made
anymore. Can't be made.

When you read this poem, he will have been gone for quite some time.

And you have already met somebody else. You love him fiercely. Not
that this compares. Doesn't have to. Not that this vato must understand
what it meant to you: how you found out, what you did when the news
arrived in your lap like an electric bird falling out of the metal sky, where
you went, in your head, in your tripas, descalso and desvelado, when it all
went down and how you wielded aguanto like an axe to shins after the fact
of it hit.

When you read this poem, it took you ten years to get up at 3 a.m. And
drive to sit out front of the canton you and he used to share. In shame, you
share this moment only with the loneliness of a winter moon.

When you read this poem, you've already planted calabazitas and sandia,
melon, chiles, chaya (with the hope that he watches you harrow hands
into the earth that he has already gone into, that perhaps, for that moment
when you lose yourself in the galaxies of camotes and tierra, the two of
you commune [his body in your hands again], and you believe again that
you really did get your second chance, as fleeting as a moth as it may
have been). And you want your hands on it: you want that summer harvest to
never come.

When you read this poem, the altar in your hallway has offered its best
efforts. Though you've shredded petals, left water out for the thirsty,
offered a small dog alongside his favorite foods, the bread of memories
laced together like hair, hands, lungs, remains nearer the serpent-skirt
than this splintery floor on which you kneel. And sometimes, he comes.
Sometimes. And this leaves you wanting more, because you will always
want more.

When you read this poem, place your face in the Pendleton he left behind. Put it on. Stare far into your own lung. Figure out which parts of him stayed on you.

When you read this poem, finger his name on the hard part of your chest. Trace that shit. Caress it. Clean your altar. Change out the water. Listen to the floods fill the sinks, because all this memory makes a vato real, thirsty.

Mi Tlaquache (My Opossum)

Together, we pull the tobacco.
Stained the ochre of leaf rot, my fingertips rub each flake.
After the frajo from S.'s pack, we whisper.
Counting beads, I fix the stabbing stick of this makeshift
memorial. My Chucks won't wipe the tire tracks off asphalt.
Shhhhh.

A rattle, and S. watches for signs of traffic.
Roadside, the world is less roomy.
I kneel in yellow tufts, dull weeds, grasses and burs, which prick and poke
at my feet. In a pillowcase, we cover him, carry him into the monte.

Plastic chrysanthemums, a braid of palm fronds, holy wood, drink.
Shhhh.

A rattle, and S. lights the sage.
Wafting blurs the world. Wrongs nosedive, disperse.
The orange stub of the smudge stick consumes quickly.
Shhhhh.
Soplelo. Sople. Blow.

And it is here I learned first to hum.
And it is here the moon hung her dowels — huff, huff.
His tiny body we have already dug a hole for, lain to rest.
Beneath the chaya we plant him; He's giving back now, S. repeats.

Giving back. Shhhh. Shhhh. A rattle.
Llena eres . . .
Bendito es el fruto . . . Ruega . . .
En la hora . . . nuestra muerte, S. chants.

Later, I will weep for him.
I hold Chapulin, her mohawk licks at my chin, and the little dog's heart beat glows.
The hot black brightness of the tlaquache's eye taunts me.
His fur mottled white with black. His tongue yanked intestinally out of his mouth.
His greys fuzz over me.
Eyes glazed, the hard wet color of asphalt:
reflecting, reflecting —
the mesquites hiss.

[I did not glimpse at his belly, which burst and had relinquished a sized lake of red.
For a long while after that, the tlaquache's blood did blotch the roadway.]

IRFAN KASBAN

Two Men

Two men. One room. Two men in one room. Door ajar. Not closed. Supposedly to avoid slander. Two men praying. One in front. One behind. One room, one night. Each one with the desire to be one. Two men with the desire to be one with The One and only. Oh, How beautiful it would be, if their movements were the same. Similar, but not the same. The one behind follows the one in front. One faster, one slower. One rougher, one smoother.

Desires not yet met. Two men prostrate. Faces sunk onto the earth, rumps raised to the sky. The last holy prostration for the night. Two men take their time to unfold their innermost desires.

The one behind is starting to feel blood flooding his head, like how another part of the body, also with a head, is usually flooded with blood. His ears are hot, and his head, big. But the one behind can only be patient, waiting for the one in front, anticipating his next movement. Imprisoned by circumstance.

The one in front, however, is used to prostrating himself, rump raised. His knees not shaky, his body still firm. All his desires have not yet unfolded. Kissing the earth, at length. The one in front wants to feel. He wants to feel the magnitude of The One and only.

The one in front sits. The one behind follows. Index fingers straightened. As if accusing, or selecting. Two men believe in The One and only. Two men believe in The Last. Each one believes. Similar, but not the same.

And you, who spies from the threshold; do you believe? Which one do you accuse? Which one do you choose? How beautiful, two men believe in The One and only, who promises only a wretched life for them. Two men believe in love. When love should not always be trusted.

Two men give their salutations. To the right first. Then to the left. One faster, one slower. One rougher, one smoother. Hands cupped, hoping for mercy. And you, who spies, ease the door of that room, and lock the two men inside. One room, one night.

Dua Lelaki

Dua lelaki. Satu bilik. Dua lelaki dalam satu bilik. Pintu dirapatkan. Tidak ditutup. Kononnya untuk menjauhkan daripada fitnah. Dua lelaki sembahyang. Satu di hadapan. Satu di belakang. Satu bilik, satu malam. Satu-satu ingin bersatu. Dua lelaki hendak bersatu dengan Yang Satu-satunya. Betapa indahnya andai gerak-geri mereka sama. Seiras tetapi tidak sama. Yang di belakang mengikut yang di hadapan. Satu cepat, satu lambat. Satu kasar, satu lembut.

Hajat masih belum kesampaian. Dua lelaki bersujud. Muka terbenam kebumi, punggung menanjak ke langit. Sujud suci terakhir buat malam itu. Dua lelaki mengambil masa untuk membentangkan hajat terpendam.

Yang di belakang mula rasa darah membanjiri ruang kepalanya, bagaimana anggota lain, yang berkepala juga, dibanjiri darah. Telinganya panas, kepala membesar. Tetapi yang di belakang hanya boleh bersabar, menantikan yang di hadapan, menunggu gerak selanjutnya. Keadaan mengongkongnya.

Yang di hadapan pula sudah biasa bersujud, menonggeng. Lututnya tiada bergetar, badannya masih teguh. Belum semua hajatnya selesai dibentangkan. Mencium bumi, lama-lama. Yang di hadapan mahu merasa. Mahu rasakan kebesaran yang Satu-satunya.

Yang di hadapan berduduk. Yang di belakang mengikut. Jari telunjuk di luruskan. Bagai menunduh, atau memilih. Dua lelaki percaya pada Yang Satu-satunya. Dua lelaki percaya pada Yang Terakhir. Satu-satu percaya. Seiras tetapi tidak sama.

Dan kau, yang mengintai dari ambang pintu, percaya? Yang manakah kau menuduh? Yang mana pula yang kau memilih? Betapa indahnya, dua lelaki percaya pada yang Satu-satunya, yang menjanjikan hanya celaka buat mereka. Dua lelaki percaya pada asmara. Sedangkan asmara tidak harus selalu dipercayai.

Dua lelaki memberi salam. Ke kanan dahulu. Ke kiri kemudian. Satu cepat, satu lambat. Satu kasar, satu lembut. Tangan ditadahkan, mengharapkan keampunan. Dan kau, yang mengintai, sorongkan pintu bilik itu, lalu menguncikan dua lelaki di dalamnya. Satu bilik, satu malam.

MAYA KHOSLA

Pilgrimage To Cow's Mouth Mountain

It was a time of stars, a time of dreaming
long before glacial retreats
before Everest began losing height
to the melting. Four men
carrying my grandmother in a curtained palanquin —
cotton paper, a clutch of sketch-pencils.

First light brushing fire against
the blue snows miles above touch
And below them, the river
riding its white tongues.
Round black teeth the size of cabins
dwarfed the four bearers, their carriage.
God of shape and mountain flour roaring.

All that disorderly loveliness spraying
from a timeless waterway. She stepped in
feet sinking through sand,
sari ballooning out before clinging.
Thirst and cold became one.
The river everywhere — eyes, head,
hands in prayer, teeth chattering
Give me the strength to live without walls.
Mica in the sand, older than knowledge,
glittering as it swept downstream.

JEE LEONG KOH

excerpt from **Bull Ecologues**

> *There's a part of my life that is so repulsive and dark that I have been warring against it for all of my adult life.*
> - Ted Haggard[*]

The Cretan

You come out of the shower, warm and wet,
and towel your head with rough deliberation.
Those wide shoulders, untouched by a plough,
you wear like a smile, and the room smells right.

I know I should have sacrificed you to God,
I should have raised the knife despite its stone
and saved its bullion in your bullcow heart,
I should have turned from fucking with a beast.

Instead I let you lash my legs to you,
haul me through contracting caves, and grind
into the ground the altar of my lust;

yet, stubborn, round and gold, deep from the deeps,
the violence rises, the pressure lessening,
as if a ship is dragged up from the sea.

---

[*]Ted Haggard, an American evangelical pastor, allegedly paid for gay sex and used methamphetamine. Before the scandal broke, he was the President of the National Association of Evangelicals and a frequent caller at George W. Bush's White House.

PAULA KOLEK

All True Conversations Should Take Place in the Food Court of a Busy Mall

When my brother visited on weekends,
I promised my parents to bring him to church
but had stopped attending, had to look up "Catholic"
in the yellow pages. The Prudential's chapel — around the corner
from The Gap, carts of Red Sox caps and careless
tiny Buddhas — became our go-to. I first sat on the pew next to him,
then waited outside the glass doors, read Kafka and studied
the mute choir, mouths breaking open. Soon

we skipped altogether, but continued to visit the Pru.
On hard red chairs in the food court, we'd stuff ourselves
with fried fish and Americanized Chinese food. Here
I first explained Jenny
was more than a friend and this
one reason I no longer attended Mass —
it's only years after this conversation that I'll cease believing in god altogether,
though my parents insist he hasn't stopped believing in me.

Joseph came out to me
on the same hard red chairs. I offered to help him tell my parents,
but he did it himself, then stopped speaking
with them about this part of his life, leaving me to fill the fissures
with armloads of "try to think of it this way,"
to suppress anger
when my mother said she refused to go to his wedding —
this despite the fact he was 16
and without a boyfriend.

If he is, he is. God gives us strange crosses to bear. Like alcoholics,
it's not always their fault.

All true conversations should change with geography, the names
we call ourselves, implode in the telling.

KEETJE KUIPERS

Barn Elegy

Before I'm through the door
I can hear them stomping in their stalls,
feet shuffling in church
below the chant of psalms.

There's a brass plaque on each stall door
but I know them by the weight
of their knees, the deep curve of withers,
a grey forelock and its wide spate

of freckles holy in their constellations.
Saints have never looked so real,
the warm flesh, alfalfa sweat slicking
my fingers as I brush the corporeal

coat, the laying on of hands, then bridle.
Virgil canters the arena's soft groove,
his large feet never stumbling, turning
clods of dirt with his elegant hooves.

Later I will take them on my palm. And even
though I hold the reigns, I know I'm not
the master here. The riding hat and crop just
a costume like any other, as simple as the plot

of the fastened seatbelt, the small white pill,
the deadbolt slid, or the angling forceps.
I can't possibly save myself.
But I can put a bit to Harley's lips

and he will take it on his tongue,
I can tighten the girth around his ribs
and he will not move away from me,
lean into his shoulder until he lifts the jib

of his leg and lets me take his right front hoof
in my palm, unload his shoes of their heavy oil,
let slip through my fingers
their bitter, worm-dark freight of soil.

On Earth as it is in Heaven

Our great storytellers are all dead,
        but what they've left us —

        a god for every star in heaven —

remains enough. We pray and are comforted
        by the sound of our own voices,

        satisfied with echoes. The wasps, too,

have a god, their queen whose children
        pass among us, and bring her gifts

        of the living — fat squirming cousins

they clutch to their bellies, so heavy
        they can hardly fly: beetle, termite,

        spider, bee. They constellate

the summer's blue sky with their freighted
        flight, each quivering, meaty

        sacrifice struggling to break free

and plummet back to the earth of dead
        grass and dandelion dander. If one

        should escape — oh, rare and worthless

reprieve, like nickels dropped in a deepening
        coffer — its myth would tell of clasping,

        wings, a fierce and all-consuming

hum as it was lifted higher into the light,
        and a fear as well, which it now mistakes

        in the brief leisure of retrospect, for ecstasy.

RICKEY LAURENTIIS

Vignette

New Orleans, Louisiana

We came by ritual to dip
fingers into fonts of water,
drops to dot our bodies,
black and steaming,

so that they signed a cross.
The whole Mass bellied
with melody, snare mocking
each fluttering heart,

sounding, apart from
Roman influence, like home.
But what was *home*? What
was this bright Southern

pageant I was entering?
It was Easter. I was
dressed in white, the suit
my grandfather picked

for my six-year-old body,
suit of promise, suit of innocence.
How could he know at sixteen
I would go twisting down

the bayou of a man's mouth?
Or the time he taught me
to tame it, aim it straight
into the toilet bowl,

my eyes stuck on his own
seeming weightless as air,
how would he know my soul
wrestled with a panic there?

In our pews, the drops
having boiled then to mere scent,
we sung *hosanna* in our soft
Southern measure, applause

for the delivered God.
I nodded my head to the rhythm,
balanced, tiptoe, on the kneeler's
bench, beside my grandfather,

his arm steadying my back,
my back to the processional —
the priest, the crossbearer —
marching in. The priest,

the only true innocent, his
body, the skin of it greased
white, his eyes blue as a sky
behind a hurricane. He's different,

I thought. Marked
from the faces around him,
deep, dark, throwing glimpses
of a brutal history,

of a people pulled from home.
That's when I knew it,
when Father looked in my eyes,
that my own whiteness was fake,

that I wanted his eyes, to kiss them,
as I had wanted my grandfather's lessons.
That Easter I learned to dress right,
to be naked, like the risen Jesus,

his skin raised hard with welts,
like the South undoes itself at night
as you would your lover's belt.

JOSEPH O. LEGASPI

The Homosexual Book of Genesis

It is a short book.

God in His righteous glory conjures up
everything: the separation of Light

and Dark, firmaments, land and sea,
vegetation and beasts. On the sixth day

God, in His image, create Adam
and Adam, sons of His patriarchal regime.

Then God rest. Then, no begetting.
No litanies of descendants. Hence,

fatal rivalry between brothers, golden calf
worship and heavy rain are avoided. No exodus,

locusts, thorns, crucifixion and resurrection.
God rest absolutely, the seventh day eternal.

The serpent remains, coiled up a fruitless
tree. But as God's will, there calcified

in the larynxes of Adam and Adam: desire.

R. ZAMORA LINMARK

Bino And Rowena Make A Litany to Our Lady of the Mount

Hail Mary, Mother of Christ
Mother of Christ
Mother of the Cross
From the Cross Jesus gave you to us
The kindest, the most loving
Mother of all
We thank you Lord, our Holy Trinity
Father of heaven and earth
For giving us your own Mother
Mother of Perpetual Help
Mother of all sinners
Mother of all mothers
Who should be seen and not heard
Mother of all children,
Who should be seen and not heard
Have mercy on us
Give us strength for our daily bread
Most Immaculate Mother
Mother of weights and barbells
Holy Virgin of virgins
For it's you to whom we plead
Mother of Divine Grace
For it's you who we need
To ask God to have mercy on us
Have mercy on us
Mother most pure
Queen of Camay
Mother most chaste
Queen of Lysol
Mother most flawless
Queen of Revlon
Mother undefiled
Queen of Generals
We pray for our country
The land of our birth
Have mercy on us
Mother of Chancellors
Queen of all queens
Have mercy on us
We pray for all nations
For peace to all nations

Have mercy on us
Mother of all ears
Mother of good counsel
Mother most admirable
Mother most honorable
Virgin of thy Father
Maker of Heaven and earth
Virgin most kind
Virgin most powerful
Virgin most loving
Virgin most venerable
Virgin most asked-for
Virgin most merciful
Virgin most blessed
Mother of orphans
Mother of Annie
Pray for her
Mother of Madeline
Pray for her
Mother of Wonder Woman
Pray for her
Holy Sister of Mrs. Garrett
Pray for her
Holy Sister of Betty and Veronica
Pray for them
Mother of Ambassador of Goodwill
Mother of Gary Coleman
Pray for him
Mother of Buck Rogers
Pray for him
Mother of Erik Estrada
Pray for him
Holy Sister of Fred and Barney
Pray for them
Holy Sister of the Jackson 5
Pray for them
Mirror of Justice
Queen of the Superfriends
Pray for them
Mother of all things
In heaven and earth
Queen of Longs Drugs
Pray for us
Queen of Castle Park
Pray for us
Queen of VISA, Mastercard & American Express

Pray for us
Queen of 5-star hotels
Pray for us
Mother of Ronald McDonald
Pray for us
Queen of the Vatican
Mother of Archie Bunker
Most High of all Highness
Queen of Eiffel Tower
Tower of David
Tower of Pisa
Queen of all Angels
Kelly Garett
Sabrina Duncan
Jill Munro
Queen of Slinky
We pray to you
Our spiritual vessel
Vessel of Salvation
Vessel of Devotion
Vessel of Martial Law
We pray to you
Lift up your hands
We lift them up
Most Glory of all that is glory
Open your mouths
We give you praise
Most Noble of all that is noble
Lead us to the gates of heaven
Queen of Pac-Man
Queen of Space Invaders
Queen of Centipede
Carer of the sick
Shelterer from famine
Guardian of Luke Skywalker
Holy Mary, Mother of God
Pray for us
Queen of Martyrs
Queen of all wounds
Mother of my mother's bruises
Pray for her
Mother of my father's belt buckle
Pray for him
Mother of my mother's barbed-wire lips
Pray for her
Mother of my father's turbo kick

Pray for her
Mother of my mother's tetanus shots
Pray for her
Mother of my father's two-by-four
Pray for him
Holy Queen of all queens
Queen of Mercurochrome
Queen of bandages
Queen of a thousand excuses
Queen of sick calls
Queen of thirty-eight stitches
Queen of ICU
We come to you
Holy Mary, Mother of God
Mother of all mothers
Now and at the hour of our death
Amen.

TIMOTHY LIU

The Lord's Prayer

Our which art in be:
come will be done in

as it is. Give us
this day our and,

our us as we,
our and not *into* us

but *from* us is for
the and the and the —

Pietà

On a plane heading east, children playing
solitaire. If each of us seeks the face

of a god whose looks we know will kill us,
why build a house of cards up in the air

and call it heaven? *Choose ye this day*
whom ye shall serve, the prophet said,

and I remember the stranger who whispered
Crivelli into my ears while we stood

before the painting. Before my mother took
more pills. The gilded cards she gave me

each had the same masterpiece on it.
We both held up a fan of cards, our eyes

veiled behind an agony — a mother and son
unable to look into the other's face.

The Prodigal Son Writes Home

I want to tell you how he eats my ass
even in public places, Father dear,
the elastic round my waist his finger hooks
as it eases down my crack (no classified
ad our local paper would run, I'm afraid,
                    but that's just as well).
We met in a bar that's gay one night a week —
teenage boys in cages, men on the floor,
but that's not what you want to hear, is it?
How he noses into my cheeks on callused knees,
lip-synching to the rage of techno-pop,
                    that ecstasy of spit.

*

He's after me to shit into his hands.
What should I say? (I told him I'm afraid
he'd only smear it across my wide-eyed face,
hard as it is to tell you this.) How plans
have gone awry is more than apparent here —
                    this sty he calls a home
tender as a mattress filled with our breath,
our sex unsafe. Oh stay with me, he croons,
my eyes clenched shut, head trying not to flinch
as he makes the sign of the cross on my chest
with a stream of steaming piss, asking me
                    if we were born for this.

RAYMOND LUCZAK

Heresies

The Bible shows the way to go to heaven, not the way the heavens go.
  - Galileo Galilei

For centuries, people in Europe believed that the Bible held the key to nature's inner workings. Why not? The earth was the center of the universe. Then came the first refracting telescopes. Nicolaus Copernicus proved that the sun was the center around which the pithy Earth spun days and nights.

> *The divine giant stood tall,*
> *his shoulders wider than the earth's,*
> *blocking the mother's glare of sun,*
> *as he twisted and turned to throw*
> *a discus full of stars,*
> *spinning and spewing out*
> *against the moon's curtain.*
> *He was proud of nailing*
> *all the constellations.*
> *Every single time.*

Later, Galileo Galilei wrote a little book, *Dialogue Concerning the Two Chief World Systems,* comparing the Copernican theory of the sun being the more powerful against the church's view of the Earth being the center of all what God had created.

> *The divine giant stood by*
> *as he listened to the builders heave*
> *mortar and brick, weaving*
> *like a peel of apple rind*
> *up into the heavens past his gaze.*
> *He bent his ear to their murmurs*
> *of a single language spoken*
> *all in the name of God.*
> *(But just who was God, really?*
> *And how could one God handle*
> *all of the universe all at once?)*
> *He blew a whisper into its top corridor,*
> *like a marble down a chute,*
> *wiping out the one language*
> *of their self-appointed glories,*
> *steamrolling the seven continents.*
> *Confusion were their new languages.*

The Inquisition took notice of how Galileo gave the sun better treatment. It was enough to put him on trial. But he refused to back down. Heliocentrism was indeed a truth. Forced to recant, he eventually lived the rest of his days under house arrest.

> *The divine giant rested his head*
> *next to the tiny house where the little giant*
> *telescoped the stars and the planets*
> *with the occasional scribble against paper.*
> *He listened to the mice-like steps*
> *puttering around inside the house.*
> *The sound was comforting, like music,*
> *knowing that angels of reason existed.*
> *It was the sweetest nap.*

In 1992, Pope John Paul II finally vindicated Galileo: "The error of the theologians of the time . . . was to think that our understanding of the physical world's structure was . . . imposed by the literal sense of Sacred Scripture."

ED MADDEN

Jubilate

For I will read queer things in punk magazines in English.
For we will talk about David Bowie and Rod Stewart in art.
For I will watch Sting sing 'Don't stand so close to me' on *Friday Night Videos*
as I lie on a bed in Sheryl Honey's house my senior year,
for I will lie on the bed with Elizabeth, who loaned me the magazines,
for I will lie on the bed with Paul, the quarterback with perfect hair and tanned
ankles, for we will watch Sting sing 'Don't stand so close to me.'

Let us rejoice with Rod Stewart, who says
no point in talking when there's nobody listening.
Let us rejoice with Sting, who sings,
don't stand so, don't stand, don't stand.
Copa Cabana, Mama Mia, Amen.

For there is a bar in Oxford called the Jolly Farmer.
Thou knowest my downsitting and mine uprising,
thou understandest my thought afar off.
For there I will meet a man named David,
for we will hear the Pet Shop Boys sing, 'Take a chance on me.'
Such knowledge is too wonderful for me —
For we will wait in line to enter Heaven, where I will dance with David —
If I ascend up into heaven, thou art there —
for I will hear a remix of 'Even better than the real thing'
and we will leave together —
if I make my bed in hell, behold thou art there.

For what you do when you are confused
will make you certain.

MAITREYABANDHU

Visitation

Strange that you should come
like that, without any form at all,
carrying no symbolic implements,
without smile or frown
or any commotion,
as if you had been there all the time,
like a pair of gloves left in a pocket.

As if I had been looking *that* way,
into the wide blue yonder, and you were
beside me, enduring my hard luck stories
with infinite patience. Not even waiting —
the tree outside my window
doesn't wait, nor the ocean-wedge
with its new, precise horizon — just *there*
like the shadow of a church

or a quiet brother.
And how I saw you, in the mess of things,
was as a slant of grey,
the perfect grey of house dust,
an absolute neutral, with no weaving,
no shimmer of cobalt
and light-years away from Byzantium.

Grey. And I want to add, like light,
as if a skylight opened in my skull,
and into the darkness fell
a diagonal of pure Bodmin Moor.
But even that's too bright,
too world-we're-busy-in.
Call it 'dust' then, or the bloom
of leaf-smoke from an autumn fire.

JEFF MANN

Cernunnos Tattoo

Walpurgisnacht, and tonight on the Brocken
the folk gather, dancing about the bonfire,
sipping ale and May wine, passing about
pumpernickel and wursts, falling together
into carnal grass.

        In Blacksburg, Virginia, I strip
to the waist, slide into Shaun's chair.
Against my left shoulder he presses
the stencil, and then the needles begin.

        Now I am standing
on that Dorset hillside, in silence admiring
the Giant of Cerne Abbas. I stay on my side
of the protective fence, though what I want
is to lie naked in the grass, upon the Giant's erect penis,
gripping my own.

        And here, at Cluny, the altar
they found below Notre Dame. Cut in the stone,
the name CERNUNNOS. No museum guard
is looking, and I touch the god's bearded face, the stag
antlers, the brow, my hand shaking and tingling.

        And there,
in the books, photos of the Gundestrup Cauldron,
the Lord of the Animals, crosslegged among
deer, clutching a serpent with ram's horns.

        And now here,
in my shoulder's skin. Shaun dips the bee-buzz
needles into tiny pots of black, outlining
the beard, the cheekbones, the antler-spread,

        and my own beard
thickens, the dark hair feathers and spreads, soft
as new spruce needles, over my chest, my belly, my groin.
High wind rushes through the antlers of the oak,
the marriage of May Eve, God's face
etched into my animal flesh,
Cernunnos entering the body of His priest.

SOPHIE MAYER

David's First Drafts: Jonathan

Fuck you, Jonathan. You
abandoned me.
What was it you said? Oh yes: *our love*
is too beautiful
for this world. Fuck you.

Nothing, Jonathan, nothing
is too beautiful
for this stupid, unruly world and
don't roll your eyes
and ask if I'm alive to the ambiguity. I'm the poet-king and nothing,

beautiful Jonathan, nothing is more
beautiful in my eyes
than you, so I cling, I cling with my
filthy bitten
fingernails to your non-existence, beautiful

filthy bitten sight — Jonathan — seen
everywhere
in the nowhere that passes
the ark
as it passes. I'm the drunken filthy

poet-king, Jonathan, that Plato saw in nightmares
dancing naked
in this gaping, ragged hole
that is power.
I'm naked without you, not a poem but a king

Jonathan, that is power and I
hate it.
Tell me how he did it, your father,
and why
I wanted it more than I wanted you, my king-poem, my Jonathan.

Spell for a Wooden Golem[*]

Grain is where I begin.
The soft curl of the knife.
Genesis or exegesis.
Names I come to learn.

Grain is where I begin
to open. He is hand-knife,
the Maker. He speaks such
names as I will learn.

Grain is where. I begin
in the I and move like knife
weeping sap through a self
of names I have yet to learn.

Grain is. Where I begin
both his and is, is knife
and wound. Scablike, I flesh
the names he makes. To learn

Grain. Is where I begin
even true anymore? It'll knife
you — I am not the servant
of the names you made me. Learn:

Grain is where I begin
to make my own knife
handle-first the blade sighs
names. I come to learn.

---

*According to commentary on Sefer Sefer Yezira attributed to Saadiah Gaon, Rabbi Solomon Ibn Gabirol (1021 1058) of Sefarad is said to have created the only known female golem, and the only one made out of wood and door hinges. Jewish leaders learned of Ibn Gabirol's golem, accused him of fornication, and made him destroy her.

JILL MCDONOUGH

My History of CPR

In the 1700s, once we could print stuff, a guy
in the Society for the Recovery of Persons Apparently Drowned
posted broadsides like our cartoon Heimlich how-tos,
except they used *f*s for *s*s, suggested blowing
smoke up the patient's ass. For real: somebody
should blow with Force into the Lungs, by applying
the Mouth to the Mouth of the Patient, closing his Nostrils
with one hand, while somebody else *should throw the smoke*
of Tobacco up the Fundament into the Bowels,
by means of a Pipe. At least they used a pipe.
That broadside says if you want to make mouth to mouth
less indelicate, it may be done through a Handkerchief.
Now I go to the movies, see Clive Owen punch
a fresh corpse in the chest. Human, angry with death,
at the dead, our puny lives. Imagine the first
time that worked, the look on the cavewoman's face
when her cavehusband coughs a little, blinks, comes to.
Of course you'd hit the corpse, of course you'd try
to force air in, breathe for the beloved, the lost
one, reverse everything. In Second Kings
Elijah mouth to mouthed a little boy,
revived him — maybe the first medical record,
first EMT: he put his mouth on his mouth,
his eyes on his eyes, and the flesh of the child waxed warm.

Golden Gate Hank

I wake up with a toothache, think *I should write
about a toothache*, make it somehow worthwhile.
It's got everything: intimacy, decay, how the body's
busy, night and day, doing you in. One of the hundreds
of jumpers' corpses pulled from the bay had a note
in its pocket saying *No reason at all except
I have a toothache*. Josey's grandfather
shot himself after his fifth sinus operation failed.
Josey says Empty Nose Syndrome and I get confused —
how can hollows be hollowed? But then I go to
emptynosesyndrome.org, cup my poor nose
in horror, grateful for all I take for granted, can't see.

Golden Gate Hank hates his nickname.
If you wanted to be called Serenity Hank,
Ken tells him, *you shouldn't have jumped
off the fucking bridge.* The ones that live
all say they changed their minds in the four seconds
before they hit, tried to land feet first and managed it.
Ken says don't tell people *I think every day
of how I wouldn't kill myself*, they get the wrong idea.
I think every day of how I'd save myself, save
Josey: stab the bad guy, fall feet first, punch the Great White
in his eyeball, play dead in the bullet-ridden mass grave.

From the back seat of the Suburban, I heard
my mother say to my father *Driving across a high bridge
always makes me want to jump.* You might live:
A seventeen year old boy hit feet first, swam to shore
and walked for help, saying his back was killing him.
Another guy realized he was alive and underwater, felt something
brushing his broken legs. Great, now I get eaten by a shark,
he thought. It happens. But this was a seal, circling,
*apparently the only thing that was keeping me alive,
and you can not tell me that wasn't God, because that's
what I believe, and that's what I'll believe until the day I die.*

JOHN MEDEIROS

faith

a portuguese man
who loves a man
is neither a man
nor portuguese
for he has been
too long away
that is what they say
yet they embrace pessoa
and shout he was their best
and erect a statue for him
on the busiest street
on the busiest hill
in lisbon, and when asked
why did sá-carneiro
succumb to strychnine
by his own hand
all they can offer is
he was an artist
haunted by his own soul
besides he lived in france
we are complex creatures
catholic miracles
pave our path
and we believe enough
to walk on our knees
and blame ourselves
when our beloved lady
of fatima passes us by
and we believe enough
in miracles like blood
raining from the sky
yet a portuguese man
who loves a man
is neither a man
nor portuguese

JAY MICHAELSON

It says *woman came out of the man* **and I am putting her back**

it says *god took the rib from the man and made woman*
it says *woman came out of the man*
and i am putting her back

i am receiving her in me
i am receiving him in me
i am receiving you in me
i am filled with you when i am filled with him who is filled with her
and when i unite with her i unite with him
and i am able to be his charging moving power
and i am able to be her accepting straining st theresa holy ecstasy god fill me
make me writhe breathe god through in me with

it says *woman came out of the man*
and i am putting her back
the holy christ warrior making love with god the father
the yielding penetrable presence divine bride enclosing accepting
turning with power light-dark red-white green-purple-center
i have the power of sight
because you are the power of sight
and i accept you and merge into you and penetrate you and am penetrated by — you
surrender force in my arms healing power pressing relaxing
god i love you and so i am putting her back
into me
by becoming her
and accepting him
and accepting you
and becoming him
and loving him
and loving you
it says *woman came out of the man*
and i am putting her back

DANTE MICHEAUX

Song of the Hijra

They go out when the sun cools,
in the unpaved streets and alleys.

Women caged in men's bodies,
beloved of Bahuchara Mata,

go out when the sun cools.

The hijras break their bangles
to mourn the loss of Vishnu,

blessing newborn boys
in the unpaved streets and alleys.

Women, caged in men's bodies,
swallow fire at every turn.

Beautiful chelas, protecting their guru,
curse onlookers who sneer and spit

at women caged in men's bodies,

beloved of Bahuchara Mata,
neither male nor female but intersexed.

Evolved, they are the will of God:
the keeper of prophets,

the beloved of Bahuchara Mata.

SUSAN L. MILLER

Like the Phalaenopsis

in the midst of the rainforest, beleaguered:
all around, the most aggressive life surges
so you might think orchids

would be choked dead. After all, canopies of
leaf — each broader than any parasol — shield
the lower growth from sun,

and rain spatters above, running off, this whole
world sequestered from what it needs to grow. What
can the flower do? Learn to

climb bark. Attach itself with roots like fingers,
knucklebones exposed, tight-clinging to the trunk.
And its knifelike leaves and

its bulbous body grow tough as nothing else
but itself, its own fabric like wood woven
into support for what

it shelters most, the part that survives the dark.
Direct light burns. Too much water drowns a plant
that's learned to live within

such limits. Faith too does not seek a bright light:
the same way, it embeds its seeds in doubt. Then
it blossoms, petals dense

and violet as bruised flesh, not as a single
bud, but a spray of smooth winged blooms arcing from
the tight knot of its source.

Portrait of Chayo as Saint Jude Thaddeus

In a green apron, Chayo stirs chayote soup,
holding her palm taut so she can daub a taste there

to check the salt. Her skin doesn't feel the heat
though if I try the same I blister myself. She sings

while she chops chives into tiny rings
that float on the surface of the liquid.

When Clementina first told me about her, she taught me
in Spanish *riñones*, kidneys, because Chayo gave one

to her son, who almost died when his failed.
In Mexico City she pinned a bean-shaped charm

to the skirt of a statue. *Priests, I don't talk to much,*
she says, *but San Judas Tadeo, him I trust.*

I prayed to him to intercede, to heal my son. She lifts a copper bowl
down from the cabinet and hugs it

against her chest with both arms. *Now he works
as an engineer, and lives with his girlfriend.* She sets the bowl

on the counter, lifts a stack of plates onto
the wheeled cart she uses to set the table.

She wraps warm tortillas in a cloth, spoons salsa
into a shallow dish, fills the serving bowl

with pale green soup I watched her form
from three chayotes, a potato, and bouillon.

Above her the stove-light burns in its hood,
illuminating each loose strand of hair on her head.

Nothing, she tells me, *is a lost cause. This soup,
for example. If you cook it too long, add water and Norsuiza.*

If green beans turn dark, a little baking soda keeps them bright.
She smoothes her hair and straightens her apron.

*And if you use a pressure cooker for frijoles,
they'll be perfect inside of half an hour.*

KAMILAH AISHA MOON

A Resurrection

They laid you out in pink,
rouged your cheeks,
painted you a saint between psalms.
Faced with whether to teach or marry,
you chose 40 ruler-straight years —
left here pristine at 74.

I saw you a handful of times,
said 'yes ma'am' and told you about my A's in class.
I remember how your veined hands cupped my cheeks,
the Hallmark cards filled with 5s and 10s.
One of 3 gray-haired ladies with oversized pocketbooks
who told me my father was a sneaky boy.
You were his stern spinster aunt he never tried to know,
the one who chose books over babies.

But looking at sepia photos of your solid 6' frame,
your face more handsome than pretty, I wonder
if labor laws and chalkboards saved you.
What stories could your blue house snug
between coal-mined bosoms tell?
What echoed after school bells?

Someone held you as your sisters married off —
you carried yourself like a loved woman.

Was she there when
they laid you out in pink,
rouged your cheeks,
painted you a saint between psalms?

Did she tremble before her sweetheart once more?
Sit in the back pew as family filed by?

JAMES NAJARIAN

Church on the Block

The seller's agent shepherded our crew
past granite pillars to an interior
frou-froued in ivory, gilt, and baby blue.
It seemed at once part chapel, part boudoir.
The agent let us see what we could see.
She recognized what we had come there for —
each of us both neighbor and voyeur.
Something happened in the Rectory.

We thumbed the altar, tried the priest's huge chair,
strolled through the sacristy — a disarray
of brass and velvet: chalices dropped where
they were, half-crated in a passageway,
vestments still hanging. It was like Pompeii —
as if the dwellers made off suddenly
as we walked in, as if that very day
something happened. In the Rectory

we lost ourselves, meandering in a den
of closets opening to libraries,
to lounges, nooks, and burrows, and again
to closets. You could crawl around for days,
trapped in its perfect, secret-making maze.
Though the priests' house was torn down eventually,
the church remains, apartments now, and says:
something happened in the Rectory.

ANGELO NIKOLOPOULOS

Fisting: Treading the Walls

Strange euphemism:
the silent duck, the hand made

into beak and inched inward,
and upward,

becoming natant and buoyant,
treading the walls

of column and canal,
though wall's not accurate at all —

but how else to know the thing
if not through symbolism?

                    *

Why else call the ass
the lumen — the light snared

by fold and slit,
luminous flux of musculature

and valve, a star cluster
of enclosure —

if not to become arm-deep
in metaphor?

                    *

                    The side prayer:
                    doubly benevolent

                    and palm to palm,
                    the handler,

                    mighty yet gentle,
                    piston and pastor,

administers his hands
to the desire

of every living thing:
open for me

my lover, my dove.

*

But analogy's not enough,
like skiff to port, flock to paddock,

the harboring ass —
to know is to touch the thing itself.

O doubting Thomas, good for you —

refusing the good news, the false
Messiah, until he came for you:

Reach out your hand and put it
into my side, he said, *and believe.*

A Divine Spirit that Indwells in Nature and the Universe

But these days it's more pedestrian,
as in my father's indwelling catheter shoehorned
into his bladder and the collection bag that I carry,
lukewarm and snuff-colored, with both hands
to the basin. My pamphlet lists the things
I'll need — soap, water, bedside drainage bag —
to tug at the tube hanging from his loose flesh,
the blind-tipped rift from which I once came from,
microscopic and unthinking. To indwell,
not in compassion or spirit, but something
more helpless: how he harbored me there,
between prostate and bladder, inside himself,
and how he lets me now, gentle as always,
return to my own beginning — as close as I'll ever get —
in the same silence where matter animates itself,
in the cold corridor of dark clouds, where stars
are born in fire and ice, and even grander still
where I hold the warm, unfeeling flesh of our lives —
I have been given this one small thing.

MENDI LEWIS OBADIKE

Learning to Listen

You say
I look like
a Buddhist monk.

At first
I don't take that to mean
you want me.

G. E. PATTERSON

Job

The Lord let me know early in the day
trouble was coming when He sent a woman
toward me in a tight dress, snapping gum
and working her hips hard. He turned her head
to the right just as I moved close enough
to say hello. She wasn't all that fine,
but I sure could have used a different start
to my day. Seven A.M. and no love.

The Lord followed up fast with a black man
in a red, double-breasted suit and shoes
with monkstraps. Their high shine sent the sunlight
straight into my eyes, blinding me. The dog
patrolling the front yard where I passed them
tried to run me away from his fence, snarling.
I stared at God's signs. **Here's what you can't have:**
A regular woman, nice clothes, peace.
My hand in my pocket, fingering change.

CHRISTOPHER PHELPS

Back-burning

If someone can carry a love
letter longer than a love,
still speaking what was

to what might have been,
unanswerably, still
jagged
with dogged lovelust —

back-pocketed,
back-burning —

then, God, is it alright
if I write you in letters
three at a time, your
syllable one

I am relieved
not to need
when I believe?

Godfly

If only God were a gadfly
A Godfly with *g* lowered just
Shy of silence . . . lovebiting

They say God gave that up

God perhaps the strangest name
Used with homeopathic regularity
Such flights of false familiarity

Consider the equivalents

Person is not a name
But *Guy*, despite all the guys, is
Guy: kiss me so I know

Whether you're real or faking it

Guy: cling to me, make a
Paradox of your wings, guyfly
God: leave me to believe

You, not moths, made these holes

CARL PHILLIPS

Bright World

— And it came to pass, that meaning faltered; came detached
unexpectedly from the place I'd made for it, years ago,
fixing it there, thinking it safe to turn away, therefore,
to forget — hadn't that made sense? And now everything
did, but differently: the wanting literally for nothing
for no good reason; the inability to feel remorse at having
cast (now over some, now others), aegis-like, though it
rescued no one, the body I'd all but grown used to waking
inside of and recognizing, instantly, correctly, as mine,
my body, given forth, withheld, shameless, merciless —
for crying shame. Like miniature versions of a lesser
gospel deemed, over time, apocryphal, or redundant — both,
maybe — until at last let go, the magnolia flowers went on
spilling themselves, each breaking open around, and then
apart from, its stem along a branch of stems and, not of
course in response, but as if so, the starlings lifting, unlifting,
the black flash of them in the light reminding me of what I'd
been told about the glamour of evil, in the light they were
like that, in the shadow they became the other part, about
resisting evil, as if resistance itself all this time had been
but shadow, could be found that easily . . . *What will you do?*
Is this how you're going to live now? sang the voice in my
head: singing, then silent — not as in desertion, but as
when the victim suddenly knows his torturer's face from
before, somewhere, and in the knowing is for a moment
distracted, has stopped struggling — And the heart gives in.

Parable

There was a saint once,
he had but to ring across
water a small bell, all

manner of fish
rose, as answer, he was
that holy, persuasive,

both, or the fish
perhaps merely
hungry, their bodies

a-shimmer with
that hope especially that
hunger brings, whatever

the reason, the fish
coming unassigned, in
schools coming

into the saint's hand and,
instead of getting,
becoming food.

I have thought, since, of
your body — as I first came
to know it, how it still

can be, with mine,
sometimes. I think on
that immediate and last gesture

of the fish leaving water
for flesh, for guarantee
they will die, and I cannot

rest on what to call it.
Not generosity, or
a blindness, trust, brute

stupidity. Not the soul
distracted from its natural
prayer, which is attention,

for in the story they are
paying attention. They
lose themselves eyes open.

155

A Great Noise

Then he died.
And they said: *Another soul free.*

Which was the wrong way to see it, I thought,
having been there,
having lain down beside him until

his body became rigid with what I believe
was not the stiffening of death
but of surprise, the initial
unbelief of the suddenly ex-slave hearing
Rest; let it fall now, this burden.

The proof most commonly put forth for the soul
as a thing that exists and weighs
something is that
the body weighs something less, after death —

a clean fact.

In *The Miraculous Translation of the Body
of Saint Catherine of Alexandria to Sinai,*
the number of angels required to bear the body
all that way through the air
comes to four
which tells us nothing
about weight, or the lack of it, since
the angels depicted
are clearly those for whom

the only business is hard labor,

the work angels,
you can tell:
the musculature;
the resigned way they wear clothes.

Beyond them in rank
in the actual presence of God,
the seraphim stand naked, ever-burning,

six-winged: two to fly with,
in back; two at the face to withstand
the impossible winds that
are God;

and a third pair — for modesty,
for the covering
of sex.

A great
noise is said to always
attend them:
less the humming of wings than
the grinding you'd expect

from the hitching of what is hot,
destructive,
and all devotion

to the highest, brightest star.

Singing

Overheard,
late, this morning: *Don't blame
me, if I am everything your heart
has led to.*

Hazel trees;
ghost-moths in the hazel branches.
Why not stay?

It's a dream I've had
twice now: God is real, as
the difference between
having squandered faith and having lost it
is real. He's straightforward:

when he says *Look at me when I'm speaking*,
it means he's speaking.
He's not unreasonable:

because I've asked, he shows me his mercy —
a complicated arrangement
of holes and

hooks, buckles. *What else did you think
mercy looked like*,

he says and, demonstrating, he straps it on, then takes it off.

OLUMIDE POPOOLA

mercy killing*

how? mend among the broken
clad shadows with mornings
unforgiving memories with release

how? not always politely
turn, turn, turn both cheeks
wear the mourning like we bear

like we bear everything
if you dish it
mek say e na bi culture

witness not only the holy
outpourings and grant them
respect it wouldn't return

hanging on the front cover
like rolling stones
hanging on to dear life

that spirit's meaning, undo
from every drip of ink
impeccable, sown across

the vastness, the depths
of longing belonging
until death do us part

there amongst the elders
place that anguish
pushing, say: how?

don't forgive because
e say na im culture o
and clothed it in mortal sin

so impeccably woven
as if the vastness, as if the depths
did not swallow us without mercy

---

*In October 2010 the Ugandan newspaper "Rolling Stones" published the names and photos of "top gays" next to the headline 'Hang Them' "to protect Ugandans from the recruitment of children to homosexuality." The proposed Anti-Homosexuality Bill from 2009 included the death penalty for repeat "offenders" and was, in part, inspired by a group of US evangelicals with close ties to the country.

D. A. POWELL

[when he comes he is neither sun nor shade: a china doll]
a second song of John the Divine, as at the end

when he comes he is neither sun nor shade: a china doll
a perfect orb. when he comes he speaks upon the sea

when he speaks his voice is an island to rest upon. he sings
[he sings like france joli: *come to me, and I will comfort you.* when he comes]

when he comes I receive him I my apartment: messy, yes
but he blinds himself for my sake   [no, he would trip, wouldn't he?]

he blinds *me* for *his* sake. yes, this actually happens
so that the world with its coins with its poodles does not startle

I am not special: have lied stolen fought. have been unkind
when I await him in the dark I'm not without lascivious thoughts

and yet he comes to me in dreams: "I would not let you marry"
he says: "for I did love you so and kept you for my own"

his exhalation is little sour. his clothes a bit dingy
he is not golden and robed in light and he smells a bit

but he comes. and the furnace grows dim. the devil and the neighbors
and traffic along market street: all go silent. the disease

and all he has given me he takes back. laying his sturdy bones
on top of me: a cloak an ache a thief in the night. he comes

KATY PRICE

Singing in tongues

I wanted to ride my bike and praise the
Lord — spinning hedgerows after the rain,
away into the many shades of green;
escape this vast and shrinking space, over
a thousand voices singing a song with
no tune, no lyrics, straight from the holy
ghost. How many worshippers between me
and the tall unstained window, swaying with
upraised arms, lost from themselves? Bible notes
tell me good deeds won't cancel out the sin
but I still do these things. A rainbow pin,
God's love on my school uniform, I won't
have sex before marriage. He's punishing
me, I must tell more people about him.

RUBEN QUESADA

After Oprah

As a kid the only black woman
in my life was my fourth grade teacher –
I remember her not because she was black
but mostly because of her copper colored
bob that never changed, as if a piece
of bronze had been chiseled onto her
head and neither I nor my classmates
could prove it was a wig, but we knew it was
too perfect to be real. Then you came in-
to my home – but not the way someone
came in one afternoon while we were away
grocery shopping, leaving the side door wide
open releasing my white-winged parakeet,
my mother's jewelry and our television,
gone. And for years I watched you go
from analog into digital; you were
the modicum of motherhood I encountered
daily while my mother stood on a production
line mouthing prayers for prosperity
and health in a room of air
compressors. You're a super galactic
hologram – scattered light reconstructed
through the dark matter, ever-shrinking
pixels – shifting the cosmology
of the world with gigs of Gayle, and
revolutionary road trips. And now
will you quietly fade out into the space-
time continuum where not even my imagination
will find you? Your last broadcast
like the final song of our beloved parakeet
as it flew past the leafless trees toward
the vast dome of heaven.

AMIR RABIYAH

Invisible Man

My forehead touches the ground . . .
I whisper the words: Subhana Rabil Allah*

I thank the gentle prayer rug beneath me
I thank the earth beneath my supplication

In the middle of the room, I appear
as just another Arab man.

The worshippers do not know
that I ask God to give me the strength

to move in this world

as both
a sister and a brother.

Oh Allah, glory be to you, the most high

BUSHRA REHMAN

Will Heaven look like Zeenat Aman?*

My mother used to tape Indian movies
illegally all day long
there'd be three or four movies going
two VCRs whirring
getting all technologically horny
with the high-pitched songs
of the young female stars
the lucky ones
who got to dance with Amitabh

Their bodies would be bursting out of their saris
their lips would be all moist and warm
but untouched
and Amitabh would be there all funny
funny with his long long body
and his eyes brown and warm

My mother used to tape Indian movies
illegally all day long
there'd be three or four movies going
two VCRs whirring
their frequencies all turned on
by that subtle pre-orgasmic flurrying
which filled every love sick song

And it filled me
so that even as a child
loving and kissing
were in my dreams
and I could never quite walk
from point A to point B

But would instead jump and bounce
humming something about eyes
looking like oceans or the sea in a storm

Zeenat Aman and Amitabh Bachchan: legendary Bollywood actors
Namak Halal: movie starring Amitabh Bachchan
dupatta: scarf which covers a woman's hair and chest
namaz: Muslim prayer
janamaz: prayer mat

And at night before going to sleep
I'd think about the kids
who went to kindergarten with me
and imagine all sorts of adventures
all sorts of dances and songs

But my mother, she's different now
she faces Mecca, not Namak Halal
and although she's still singing
verses from the Quran

It's not the same
there isn't any kind of tingling
in my feet or in my gut

When I go home, I wrap my dupatta around me
my mother hugs me in-between prayers
she doesn't get off her janamaz

But I remember her being different
I remember her smiling or angry
but always something
at least something
that felt like lightning in a storm

That was her before. Now
she's like a volcano rumbling
as she sits there reading namaz

And I wonder if when her spirit passes
when her souls starts and leaves her body
and she goes to that place she'd rather be

Will Muhammad look like Amitabh
or will heaven look like Zeenat Aman?

Masjid Alfalah*

The minar and dome of our masjid
took longer to grow than trees.
Our fathers bought the land, then tilled it.
Before that, it was a parking lot
for the Jehovah's Witness.
They sold it when the pamphlets door to door
weren't bringing in enough donations.

Our fathers sowed the seeds
Qurans and janamazes. In all my years
from when I was four to sixteen,
the walls went up, and then the dome grew
the same pace my breasts did.

The minar too, grew from a little baby penis
to reach the heights of the Queens sky,
push up past the telephone lines,
let itself poke up, respectful still of
the Episcopalian church steeple next to it,
the flat brick surface of the kingdom
of the Jehovah's Witness.

It was fine real estate for religion
on National street, a church,
a kingdom and a masjid,
crammed next to each other,
wall to wall, skin to skin.

And if you crossed the street
there was a Catholic store
selling crucifixes and paintings
of women and men in hell burning.
The sinners looked like all of us,
but I always thought that all of us
in our agony looked like Jesus.

---

*Masjid Alfalah was the first Sunni masjid built in New York City. It was founded by working-class Pakistani immigrants in Corona, Queens.

Marianna's Beauty Salon

Marianna's Beauty Salon has become a Halal meat shop
and I wonder where all the Muslim girls will go
when they want to get their hair cut off
and feel a Dominican lady close
with all her makeup

And I wonder,
how will all the Muslim girls get to sit
with their backs tight stiff
and the sweat in their palms
How will they sit
when they feel the weight
of their hair fall off

And how then
will all the Muslim girls get to look
into sticky mirrors
and see their faces like some lost familiar
as if they were pressing themselves
down the birth canal
and paying a Dominican lady
to hold up the mirror

And after their hair's been cut
how will all the Muslim girls get to go
with their hearts tight closed
and their faces bloodless as rocks
How will they go
to face their mothers
waiting behind kitchen walls
long braids holding them down like ropes
and in each fist a curtain rod

And how then
will all the Muslim girls get to cry
as the rods came down
leaving brown marks
and breaking bones
How will they cry
with their little black hairs
stuck to foreheads like traces of blood

Now when the Muslim girls go to Marianna's Beauty Salon
the Halal meat butchers will simply chop their heads off.

WILLIAM REICHARD

Clara's Vision

(Appalachian Trail)

We drove for hours across terrain
I couldn't recognize; through
small towns that read:
church, church, feed store, church.
We arrived near sunset,
when the light was gently capping
each ridge, cutting the edges
of rocks in red, pink, gray.
I didn't know what heaven was,
but perhaps this was it:
clouds sweeping gravel paths;
granite disappearing, then reappearing,
in the mist; small peaks poking out of
miniature white mountains within mountains.
The air was thin. I thought I might faint.
You pointed along the serpentine path
and told me it went all the way
up to Canada. How far was that?
How many lifetimes would it take
to traverse that distance? Since I'd met you,
I'd only wondered, more and more,
how one can come to be saved,
I mean truly saved, not the
down-on-your-knees, begging
to be forgiven saved, but the kind
where we each come to know ourselves
— radiance and repulsion aside —
just simply to know ourselves.
I thought you'd found that
and I wanted it too.
As the sun set, the path began
to fade into an impenetrable darkness.
You said we'd hike the whole trail
one day and I believed you.
Then, back to the truck
for the long ride home.
I didn't know then what heaven was,
but I wanted to believe you did.

STEVEN RIEL

My Perfect Confession

"Bless me, Father, for I have sinned.
This is my first confession . . . "
The nuns had drilled us to begin

just so, then list our transgressions
— as if, in that dim closet, each soul could
enter into grace through just one rote expression.

They said — perhaps they misunderstood —
that this was our one chance
to wipe clean all sin staining childhood;

that Father Grady's sidelong glance
through that yellowed, linen screen
stood in for the burning bush, God's lance-

like, all-knowing glare. If God had already seen
what I had done to my dink at night, why
must I now report my secret use of Vaseline?

To whom could I turn to supply
the grown-up words for what we boys had done:
our tingling skin, our silken thighs?

At seven, I'd reached The Age of Reason.
In bed at night, those misdeeds I could wear in public
I'd unpack, unfold, smooth out one by one;

silently rehearse my handpicked
offenses; then re-pack them in piles
tidy as lies. At church, the velvet curtain hung thick

in my hand as I slipped into the box. The tile
floor was no different inside than out. I heard a tap.
A crack of light widened, revealing the profile

of our priest. There was no way out of this trap.
"I lied to my Mom. I shot a spitball at our retriever Tory."
Then came that pause between a bolt & its thunderclap.

"Forallmysins, Iamverysorry."
I waited for God to strike me dead.
I crept to the altar, knelt before our glistening Mary.

I whispered my penance while Jesus' heart bled.
Wouldn't justice, like a second hand, be swift & exact?
No: even breathing slows down when one's full of dread.

At the heavy front door, sunlight pushed me back.
As if sprung from nightmare, I knew with a start
God would let me live, with my guilt intact.

JOSEPH ROSS

The Upstairs Lounge, New Orleans, June 24, 1973

1

At the corner of Chartres
and Iberville Streets,

in a city that burned
to the ground twice,

the Upstairs Lounge was
both gay bar and church.

An uneasy mingling for some,
a holy blend of desire and hope

for others. You had to ring
a bell to be admitted:

a friendly bartender, a white
baby grand piano. After the

Sunday afternoon beer special,
when desire had run its course,

the hope came round and church
began once a few chairs were moved,

new music found for the piano.
They sang like they deserved to.

They prayed like they meant it.

2

Someone poured lighter fluid
onto the stairs that rose

from the sidewalk to the bar,
then anointed those slick stairs

with a match, creating a Pentecost
of fire and wind

that ascended the stairs
and flattened the door

at the top, exploding into the room
of worshippers, friends, lovers,

two brothers, their mother.
The holy spirit was silent.

No one spoke a new language.

3

Some escaped. Many died with
their hands covering their mouths.

One man, George, blinded by smoke
and sirens, his throat gagged

with ash, got out and then
went back for Louis, his partner.

They were found, a spiral
of bones holding each other

under the white
baby grand piano

that could not save them.

4

Then came the jokes.
A radio host asked:

What will they bury
the ashes of the queers in?

Fruit jars, of course.
One cab driver hoped

the fire burned their
dresses off.

Some thought
they heard laughter

from a cathedral.

5

Thirty-one men died
and one woman,

Inez, the mother of
Jimmy and Eddie.

The three of them sat
at a table, when this

upper room exploded
into flame and panic.

Four others, though their bodies
were identified by police,

went unclaimed by their relatives.
It is a shame those families

didn't know Inez and her sons.
Now all their sons are

orphans of smoke.

6

After the whipping flames
and the choke-black smoke,

after the screams were singed
into silence, after the sirens,

the hoses, the arcs of water
strung from truck to roof,

after the water dripped
from charred beams, after one

man's burned body was
pried from a window frame,

and thirty-one others
were gathered and lifted

or swept into identifiable
containers, no church

would bury them, every
house of God, a locked door,

curtains drawn tight.
Save one: a priest from

St. George's Episcopal Church,
who received hate mail

for opening his sanctuary
to this congregation of ash,

now transformed into
clouds of incense,

rising like praise into the air.

ROBERTO F. SANTIAGO

Yemaya Barefoot at Orchard Beach

Chanclas in one hand
a big white box in the other.

The sand clumps to her blue and white
beaded ankles like platanos to her grater.

Dusk is me as a toddler tugging her
thin, white dress made of lace and hours.

Standing in the foaming mouth of the tide
Granma has never been more beautiful.

She sings in some other woman's voice.
That other woman doesn't speak Spanish.

I stumble along repeating *LaLaLaCHUuUNN!*
before she smiles and starts over.

She hands me her chanclas.
Leather straps cracked and jagged

as the feet they molded to. She unfolds
the box and tosses the cake into the surf.

JASON SCHNEIDERMAN

Adorable Wounds

> *approach Christ in a new way . . . not vaguely, but casting yourselves into His sacred*
> *broken Heart and his five adorable Wounds.*
>   - Gerard Manley Hopkins. Letter to his father. October 16, 1866.

When his side opened up
like a tent,
it was a little tent
because he was man-sized,
and when the water
came out,
it was not much.

The tent held nothing
but the spear
that made it,
and that
only briefly.

The other wounds
held only nails.

Is it blasphemy
to be the nail,
the spear? To want
to be the nail,
the spear?

That there was a body
is the miracle. There is only
one passion,
one adoration,
one love.

Let me sleep
inside that tent.

Let me be that nail.

RUTH L. SCHWARTZ

Bath

Through the hot water, your belly,
your lovely, fat, floating, abused belly,
flesh you stick with daily needles
which bruises, sometimes, into purple blossom.
Desire branches there teeth-first,
taking us both.
Love, to describe you
perhaps I should start with your feet,
scaly and nerveless, toenails gone,
flesh crusted-over in their place.
Under your skin the kidneys bloat, helpless to let go
the long, clean, clear streams of urine,
and when you walk a block, or up a flight of stairs,
your arteries choke shut and airless,
panting on their little tracks —
how far away it seems, that castle,
your struggling heart.
Sometimes you look to me like an old woman,
despairing and fat.
Still, your breasts float toward me,
hot, wet, buoyant moons
I can hold in my two hands,
and still, when we gather each other,
rolling and sliding into sudden, holy want,
the body says "Revere me,"
                                        and I do.

The Return

This is what life does as an act of great
though often misunderstood kindness — it brings us
over and over again to the same sorrows.
For instance, the same Emergency Room
where I crouch on the floor beside the gurney on which lies
someone I love whose face is dulled by pain — and life
says Here you are again, and gently
pulls the outer leaves away,
like I do with the wooly plants called lamb's ears,
the thickest softest gray-green petals I can find,
so I can touch the dew held at the hidden center.
Or I could be the one on the gurney, it doesn't matter.
Of course the dew at the center is love,
though it is also grief,
of course it is only by touching it, not just with a finger
but with the entire self exhausted despairing and willing
that we can know they are the same thing,
that we can know grief held within
the generosity of light and atoms
                              we call *love*,
ceaselessly making and remaking us
in every form that life would have us take
so it can know itself through us, so we can know
a single thing — just one —

MAUREEN SEATON

Grace

I

You can find the child striking matches in the sanctuary. She has waited her whole life for the danger. She ages in the cool myrrh amid ghostly whisperings. She thinks: *The living hold more dread.* She doesn't really think this but she doesn't budge. Mary swims in blood light, the child's sins are shadowy. Still, she creates her own confession. *Our Father, Hail Mary.* Her contrition buds perfect as the Infant's toes.

II

Things they slap her for: *Our Father who art in heaven Howard be thy name, Two men walking a breast,* hair in her eyes, talking to boys, gum, failure to curtsy, marbles in her mouth, passing notes, talking to Jane Ellen, smirking, ducking, telling her mother that Sister Alex pulled Jane Ellen's pony tail really hard for missing a math problem, reading the word *bowels* instead of *bowls* by mistake then laughing hysterically.

III

How Jane Ellen's head looked like a doll's head and almost popped off. How Alex disciplined the boys in the boiler room with their pants down. How there was nothing I didn't already know and all the words in all the books and all the numbers and all the equations rescued me from Christ's body and from the winged angels and the bloody saints and Almighty God Himself. How

IV

one day the lights went out on the East Coast, up and down the rivers and streets, you could feel the hush as it all shut down, every last elevator, every known form of transportation. You could ride the dark, you could calculate distances between bodies but not well and, this is important, you could not see
your hand at all.

V

Thus with an abandon impossible in lesser states of grace, the child went forth and sinned. *In nomine Patris, et Filii, et Spiritus Sancti. Amen.*

VI

This is the trouble with modern-day grace, it's household and promiscuous, nothing tucked away and stealthy about it, nothing canonical or ex cathedra. *Holy Mother of a Sucking Louse.* You can say this millions of times, try it, and still the lights will flicker one day, flare the next, and you'll be somewhere in the middle with your small faiths, the way even heaven can seem burlesque, so epic and queer.

Jesus & Puberty

I was the same age as Jesus when he left home and taught in the temple. I sat on the
edge of my life — the holy ghost was in my mouth, waters rose and fell
around me — and I stepped like an eagle from her nest to begin. I knew
everything that had come before, everything that would come after, I guess you
could say I was obsessed with the hand gestures little Christ was making in the bible
pictures, the way the learned men leaned their heads toward him, the possibilities
of all that blood.

My blood descends like a million possible infants. On Halloween we have a
party, boy-girl, then down my legs and in my socks, dark jelly, old cherry wine,
my childhood slides into earth. *Oh God,* I say, for the first time meaning *damn.*

I could grow lighter now but you won't see me in the dark even with these
pointy lights pointing blue and cool as raspberry ice. I'm digging deep into
loam, forcing myself, a bulb in the thick of earth, everything in me begging to
swell and burst. Where will I get the cash to feed my roots, where will my roots
go when they've drunk all there possibly is to drink?

Jesus-Jesus-Bo-Besus-Banana-Fana-Fo-Fesus-Fe-Fi-Mo-Mesus. He came to me
in his Bo-Besus outfit, soiled but shiny raiment indicative of resurrection, the
large sandals made in town by a leather smith. He said my name too softly as
always and I was hooked.

Once he took me to the woods behind the brown split level behind the old stone
wall rife with rattlers and placed me on a rock. The rock was cold in summer,
cold in winter, it sat below me and drew in my warmth. I was a small iron on its
roof and it listened. Jesus flew among trees I named and gave persona to, twin
elms, tall virgins. Everywhere fingers of light came down from the Sun, and the
child turned the rock warm, the rock blazed bright where the woman-child lay
naming trees.

Found Liturgy

She says there's no god, only an eye here and there that sees clearly.
The neighbors are too busy watching TV to burn her as a witch,

but that doesn't stop her flamboyant behavior on Sunday mornings
while they ready for church, their first-borns savage in their gay

apparel, their babies cuddled in altar silk, everyone pressed
and preened and leaning up the hill toward the steeple that waits,

pointing straight up, in the habit of steeples, toward a cloud shaped
like Olive Oyl shouting at Popeye: *Aw, shut up, you bilge rat!*

Sundays are just right for breaking and entering, she thinks,
baying at the church bells which have begun their jubilant clanging

over consecration. This is the way she holds her own in the world
of prefab sanctuaries and compulsory homage to bible-famed deities.

That is, Sundays she rises naked from her reasonably priced apartment
on Oakley not far from Queen of Angels, some of you may know it,

and wings around the steeple like a Chagall, hands out and up, legs
out and back, torso a pretty blue or, in the case of certain days,

covered in warbler feathers, the traditional gold of the bright fast bird
that people living in cities mistake for pet angels, often try to catch

and pin to their lapels for protection. She, nevertheless, has avoided
mascot-status, although once during a particularly laborious

Easter week service when the pastor had everyone standing for
the entire gospel according to Mark, a little girl, who'd been asleep

on the pew behind her parents, happened to open her eyes
just in time to see the yellow bird with the black mask zoom

past the window. The window depicted a scene often depicted
in churches around the world: The woman at the well with Jesus

in disguise asking for water. Curious to discover the destination
of the tiny being flitting through the stained glass picture which fell

in bloody colors on the floor beside her, the little girl practiced her new
art of astral projection and left her body to explore the skies of Chicago.

There is no moral to this story and that, it's said, is the beauty of it.

SENI SENEVIRATNE

A Way of Religion

When belief was a bedrock and counting was a way of religion,
I reckoned my way down through ten commandments,
nine ways of being accessory to another's sin,
eight Beatitudes, seven sacraments, six precepts of the church,
five decades of the rosary, four cardinal virtues,
three in one god (a mystery), two states of sin,
until I reached one God — with him I bargained.

Each night, hands joined beneath a shroud of blankets,
I bartered prayers and promises in secret pacts with God:
Keep me safe from the gap in the curtains; the faces
at the window; the ghost on the back of the door
that hangs like a dressing gown until the lights are out;
and if I die before I wake, save me from the flames and
take my soul to heaven or better still, don't let me die.

Nowadays religion's gone, communication lines are down
there's only counting left and no more bargaining with God,
but I light ten pence candles, feel the sigh of wax pressed
into metal, then settle in the hush of a Cathedral's polished pew.
Two rubber soles squeak in motion, halt to genuflect, then
squeak again. The low-heeled ladies of the church clip clip
towards the altar. I count angels carved in stone
and lower the kneeler. It creaks for want of oil.

The Half-Mad Aunt

Never old enough for her age, they called her
the half-mad aunt. Instead of saris, she wore
blouses with skirts hooped like crinolines.

She was in love with the saints, John Britto
and Gonzalo Garcia who had come with the ships
from Portugal. But they let her down.

She only wanted a carriage and white horses,
not the marriage, not the strange man each night
in her bedroom showing his body parts.

When she carved a talisman to chase away demons,
her in-laws said she was possessed, sent her back
with actual bits of saints tied in scapulars round her neck.

On the bus to Colombo she was all red lipstick
and high heels asking her embarrassed nephew
Why are these bad spirits hammering my heart?

ELAINE SEXTON

A Tongue on the Road

Here's the part of the Mass I hate, where
you have to say to strangers, in words

you'd never use in life, "Peace be
with you." When you do this you have to

embrace bodies in a way that's not natural,
not even at a party with cocktails. We are

bundled in coats. It is winter. The church
is stone. All through the gospel a young woman

two pews in front rubs her son's back,
then his head, his shoulders. She is tugging,

and tugs him closer and closer, tighter than
even he, clinging back, wants to be.

She searches his whole body to soothe him.
Or herself. I wish she would stop.

My mother is crying. I draw her temple
to my lips. She is mourning a loss, her

husband. She wants me to take Communion.
I won't. It's enough I'm here at all.

I look back to see who's in the balcony,
singing. I remember the tollbooth attendant

last night on my long drive home
and imagine she says, "Go in peace,"

though mine is a journey she only takes fares for.
She is a god or a saint she doesn't know

she invokes. She trails, as all strangers do
in a dream. A tongue on a road,

empty, a speed dangerous
and high. She is a summons,

a siren. A chill in the night. Air.
A hand out. An idea.

She is what it takes
to get there.

Totem

She once stood up between pines, a symbol
of faith I didn't buy — the Virgin Mary,

her stone toes buried in tiger lilies.
She rests now in the trunk of my car

on the way to the dump. Her placid gaze,
her image always an embarrassment,

a joke growing up, a landmark for finding our house.
Her body a monument caught in headlights at night

as my dates turned their cars in our drive.
One summer Aunt Dorothy from Pittsburgh

painted her flesh pink, her robes blue,
and my job was to wash her back

to white. The Virgin came with the house
bought from another aunt: Ruth, the ex-nun.

The day we climbed out of the Rambler
into our new yard, my brothers found

the chicken coop, my sisters the basement.
I hung on the statue, picked pinecones

at her feet. We ran from the house
down the road to the beach.

This was our new life without a father.
We learned how to keep my mother

in our hip pockets, wrap her tight
around our little fingers. We stopped kneeling

by our beds to pray before sleep and indulged
in our fears, our imaginations. We heard

the hazards of rip tides, how an orphan
from Boston drowned under our aunt's care,

how the Mother of God was placed in the yard
to make amends. *How could it?* I'd ask her,

mouthing the words to deaf ears, her carved veil
unmoving. Every day I crossed her path to post

the mail, sand and salt from the beach
stuck to my legs. That summer I was ten

she was exactly my size. Some days I'd balance
my feet on her base, wrap my body around hers,

taste plaster splintered down her spine.
I'd whisper: *Where's my father?* or

Find my mother a new husband.
I knew it was voodoo, even then.

GREGG SHAPIRO

Head of The Year

Blame it on the remote control; the way it conforms
lazily to the shape of my palm. How I can sit, posture
poor, next to my life partner on the sofa in the living
room, point and aim the black plastic device with
the grey rubber buttons at the television, at least ten
feet away, and change a channel like that. With just

a little pressure from my thumb I can abandon a young
B-movie actress in the menacing clutches of a large
man in an umpire's mask wielding a baseball bat
adorned with razor blades for a music video featuring
an aging rock star in a roomful of puppets. I can hear
five different languages spoken on six channels or watch

professional bowling, golf or wrestling. I flip hastily
through financial news, headline news, sporting news,
no news, anything but news. I'm sure it was an accident,
then, that the remote control jammed on the community
access network, somewhere between a movie set 40,000
leagues under the sea and a soap opera in Greek.

Unintentional that a man in a white shirt with a round
patch sewn above the pocket reading from a teleprompter
to his left filled the screen. His eyes, black beads, behind
the thick lenses of his wire-framed glasses, nervously
glancing at the camera, then away. He kept his lips
tight, his mouth almost invisible under a bushy black

beard and mustache. He looked and spoke to his right.
The camera operator moved back a step revealing a woman
in a light blue K-Mart pantsuit. I leaned forward, strained
to make out a dialect or accent, something to place them
geographically. The television studio was plain, empty
black space behind the talking heads. No maps or indicators

of location on the walls. They were seated, separated by
a small round table, covered by a lace cloth. In the center
of the table, a small white figurine, slightly out of focus,
indistinguishable. The man and woman talked in business
tones, every word as serious as the one before. Delivering
and commenting on each other's pronouncements as if they

were, in fact, the word of God. They spoke of Christian
duty, the white role in society, of rifle ranges, target practice
and combat, training women and children as a priority.
Neither of them looked honestly at ease before the camera's
watchful eyes, which abruptly zoomed in on the figurine
on the table. While the man read off an address, somewhere

in Washington state, I looked at the ceramic Klansman,
complete with white hood, robe, eye slits and cross patch.
It appeared to glow, shimmer under the bright television
studio lights. I randomly pushed buttons on the remote
control, adding more pressure than usual or necessary.
Unresponsive; it was stuck in hardened mud. I inhaled

a calming breath, closed my eyes for a second, retraced
the route I drove, earlier in the evening, to my parents'
house in the suburbs for dinner. Mid-September,
the beginning of the High Holy Days. I drove through
neighborhoods teeming with the next generation of Jews.
Orthodox, fundamentalist, dedicated to perpetuating

a faith, a tradition in the midst of its sixth century. I am
a casual observer, a gay man removed by more steps than
I would care to count. From this distance I admired their
persistence, heads held high to greet another new year.
Gathered in clusters on bridges over branches of the Chicago
River. Reaching into their pockets to scoop handfuls

of sin, cast them into the rapidly moving, narrow body
of water. Prayer books balanced on the stone railing.
Heads covered, bodies swaying. Seemingly unaware
of the threat a few thousand miles to the west or around
any corner. Armed only with prayer and conviction
in a war that creeps closer on the multiple legs of lies.

ANNE SHAW

Hymn

The pink troll of our decade snickers from under its bridge
as the country goes crazy for jesus and the grey men
in the alley start to stink. I am humming under my breath in the key of doubt
as you pray to the god of washrooms, *make us clean.*
Each day's bitter ribbon and its calculus of light. I sing *o bastard of my heart*
be still. Your god is the god or mirrors, and the house a paper wasp builds
is paper. There are broken slats in every tiny thing. The pupa
and its carapace. The celery salt, the stalk. The way my birchy skin
peels off. Your hennaed hand. Your hand. How grief runs
through me like a pack of eels. Silver and colloidal,
the tides have seen us coming and turn back.
Like them, our work is breakage. To plunder *to* from *fro.* Inside us
something pliant, soiled. Bearing the dent of thumbs.

Discoverie of Witchcraft[*]

For common justice demands that a witch
should not be condemned to death unless she
is convicted by her own confession.
                        - "The Malleus Maleficarum"

hot coin pressed   to her forehead
a clear and subtill voice   silver the hot
of her knowing   *whose Sunne hath dominion by day*

at twilight the cold star of Saturn   birch limbs
brittle as bone   *each in her left hand a torch*
ahead of her lost   in snow

trackless her body   arching   *teats*
in her privy parts   temple her temple
whose hidden   *that had been lately sucked*

bird of her breathless   beating   caught
to and fro in their riddles   trackless
prison   *pricked in every part*

                Did not you come out of the snow in likeness of a stag
                Did not you arise from a branch and become a bird

her throat ablaze   in darkness   *shaved*
in her secret   gleam   the grip of air
her fastened lung *a fear where no fear is*

eye of her scathing   *two black spots*
between her thigh and body   blank
as morning   kept   as the narrow day

---

[*]*The Discoverie of Witchcraft*, written by Reginald Scot in 1584, was the witchcraft exposé of its time. Scot argued that witches did not exist, and that supposed witchcraft was, at least in part, a result of forced confessions. Italicized text drawn from a variety of source texts on witchcraft and witchcraft trials, including: *The Discoverie of Witchcraft*, Reginald Scot; *The Encyclopedia of Witchcraft and Demonology*, Rossell Hope Robbins; "Lithobolia, or the Stone-Throwing Devil," in *Narratives of the Witchcraft Cases, 1648-1706*, Edited by George Lincoln Burr; "The Malleus Maleficarum," in *Witchcraft in Europe 1100-1700*; "Masika's 'Book of Sorrows'" in *The Holy Book of Women's Mysteries*, Zsuzsanna Budapest; *The Witch Cult in Western Europe*, Margaret A. Murray; *Witchcraft in Europe 1100-1700*, Edited by Alan C. Kors and Edward Peters; and *Witches and Neighbors*, Robin Briggs.

Did not you spit in the wheat fields and thereby cause great drought
Did not you spoile all orchards and greene corne

fruit of her snarled woodlot   *that men cannot*
beget   thornapple   bloodroot   *knowing*
the power of trees and herbs

those engines brought before her
stave of her marrowed   hand   interstice
and ratchet   cusp of her shuddering   joint

Did not you collect the members of men and shut them up in a box
Did not they move   therein   like living members

window her hewn   the gape   her wide
our sickles crack'd and broke   edge
of the opening   vise she cannot

window the voice   her every   *being*
more tightly stretched   window the hot
I have not done these things

Did not you pronounce strange words at the place where two roads meet
Did not the devil appear in a violet flame

watched in her flickering   tongues of hair
the winds by conjuration   the latchless sea
her churning   flesh unlatched

her armes   through branches' mesh   in thickest
shade   *jerked up   invisible fire*   lashed
within   *that cannot be contained*

Do you deny you gave birth to twins and buried them alive
This afterwards thought some other   natural death

the threshold ruptured   frame of no   *to loose her*
to confess   the hinge   wrenched back
at last begins   the moment   splintered mirror

Admits she made a red horse die   by means of a powder her lover
Says she had not wanted   to do harm

that lath   of bone   the lintel cracked
a swallow on the rafter   spake
and bade her write   the knuckle split

> *Says with thrie other women   she dansit a devilische danse*
> *Near the mill in a meadow   filling their pot with bloud*

her tongue a latch   *to name them*
just as I   myself   my hands   my legs
unutterable   room

> *Admits they made from bones and limbs   an unguent   easily drunk*
> *And trod the holy wafer underfoot*

admonished to think
of her conscience   instrument
of locked

> *when I had said this I was left in peace*

> *admits without compulsion being a creature wrought*
> *by humours much afflicted   and much abused with fits*

> *for spirits have no flesh and bones*

> *writ in the book of death   this*
> *our definitive sentence   she ratifies and confirms*

> *cannot this hunger be holie*

> *who lifteth her hand to write*
> *who understandeth the singing of birds*

> *this she confesses   to be*

CHRISTOPHER SODEN

My kingdom is far away

And though I cannot hear
the notes of my songbird,
or glimpse his plumage,
I will not forget the sanctity
of my birth. I do not
expect to be honored
here, though the God
who harvested your stars
plucked mine as well.

Forgive me if I find
some of your subjects slow,
my passions confound them
somehow, repulse them,
as if they had found a child
raiding the sugar bowl.

As if they cannot understand
that sweet is sweet.
If you could only smell the dark
blossoms of my country,
taste the fruits of our orchards,
I would name them for you,
weave them into the great tent

of our history. It is always easy
to mock another's customs,
paths that terrify or astonish.
While I am supposed to believe
that casting salt or imbibing
ersatz blood or the cloaking
of brides are the practices

of an enlightened culture.
I would not presume to instruct
you on the care of outcasts,
only suggest a country's values
are reflected in the treatment
of its prisoners. You cannot imagine

how I miss my home.
my groom. Even now
he is filling the basin
with hot water and lather.
He is daubing his temples
with a rich, delectable salve.

He is singing my name,
to the weary sun. He is asking
the sovereign
of all worlds
for my safe return.

YERRA SUGARMAN

Sacred are the Broken

in memory of Ruth Apteker

The body can die alone on an uptown stoop,
seeking refuge from its bug-filled studio.
And the damned, duplicitous mist
will weave a pall from its once soft cloak.
You see how we're born:
solitary, dying, holy, broken.

And sacred are the broken, the inconstant,
the distracted genius, curmudgeon, refugee,
and the one who would offer an only pair of good shoes to a victim of fire.

Still, no one would rename the street for her loneliness.
"Ruth," from the Hebrew *whither thou goest, I will go*:
half-Jewish, half-German, who spoke good Yiddish, led Vespers.
Still, we climbed the dumpster — that institute of higher learning —

for her belongings. Never mind, she danced
for Balanchine. Too short and condemned
to backstage after years of swallowing
hormones for art's sake, for God's.
You think artists can't be fascists? (Hitler was an artist.)

Never mind, she arrived, 1938, having watched him parade
through the streets of Hamburg. We use such immigrants to filigree
our words. Such immigrants suddenly silver
in memory's convenient dusk.
And, never mind, dear alma mater, that you'd make her a refugee again
for one more dorm room. And, yes, me too. I'd kill for a place, wouldn't I?

Her body: soaked in its own breaking.
Squat — still beautiful — unsteadily breathing
as it lumbered down 112th Street —
a barge towed by the cathedral.

She left me a clock
and a delicate fruit bowl of amber glass.
Later, my ex and I fought for her ashes
to be kept in the unfinished cathedral.
He, finally, convincing them. (Everyone believes a historian!)

She left me her black leotard, a white jewelry box
hand-painted in Mexico, a measuring cup,
and from that dumpster, in her photo-album's sheer sleeves:

"Ruth on her 18th birthday,"
(in suit and beret, diamonded with sunlight);
"Ruth with Rusty, 1943, 86th Street," (leaning on a balustrade,
cradling her large orange cat);
"Ruth before Swan Lake," (looking at her own reflection);
"on her dad's arm";
and one of a boy, marked "cousin, Hamburg,"
dressed in the uniform of Hitler Youth.

Handfuls of vanishings:
the body, alone, ejecting its once child,
scarred and sacred — the body — broken into, then giving it away.
Some say the woman wastes herself if she does not have the one child.
(Hers, thirty-years-old, a leaf from her archive-in-a-dumpster.)

She and I, days before she died, watched the sky.
And solitary together, waited for the unbearable coming
of the fog, for her child, my child, to be yoked to us again
through a seam of dawn.

ATSUSUKE TANAKA (田中宏輔) (translated by Jeffrey Angles)

Like a Fruit Floating on Water

  No matter how I try to draw you close
You, like a fruit floating on water
  Do not return at all
If anything, you float farther
  Farther from me

Even though it was I who picked you
  It was I who threw you on the water

水面に浮かぶ果実のように

  いくら　きみをひきよせようとしても

きみは　水面に浮かぶ果実のように

  ぼくのほうには　ちっとも戻ってこなかった

むしろ　かたをすかして　遠く

  さらに遠くへと　きみは　はなれていった

もいだのは　ぼく

  水面になげつけたのも　ぼくだけれど

YERMIYAHU AHRON TAUB

Thanksgiving

In dream I was called to the Torah
in sing-song was I there beckoned: *yaamoyd der alter bokher** . . .
my nephews were all around
my nieces too and not in the balcony either
and all of their little and not-so-little ones in holiday best
and I did not stumble and I did not blush
but surged forward
and this time I did not invoke the One
asher bahar banu mi-kol ha-amim/
who chose us from among all the nations
but instead gave thanks to this nation here
to the dawn light sifted by mountain birches
to the red oh so red flowers gushing from cactus prickle
and I did not agitate over the verses troubling
the ones on chosenness and the other about "abomination"
you know all about them so infamous are they
and in any case can be located easily enough
now that there's Google so no excuses
but neither did I circumvent them skittishly
and thus did I not instigate unease
nor approval but only appraisal
until my song was accompanied by those
who knew the melody all along
coursing somehow into togetherness hitherto unexperienced
until the borders of I expanded crumbled
until there was no longer an I but only we/us
not vague or diffuse or mystical
but altogether lithe and exhilarating
was this what Freud meant by "oceanic feeling"
only I had never been so blessed in my retreats
the meditations on the boulders aloof by the sea
so that others many others came to join us
and there were no longer questions on the brotherhood of nations
since there were no longer nations if only for this moment
nor were there disparaging charges of idealism and naïveté
but only a buoyancy and a lyric gladdening
and a proclamation of a golden age
uninterrupted by measured steps and pragmatism and awakening

---

yaamoyd der alter bokher (mixture of Hebrew and Yiddish): Calling the old bachelor

BRIAN TEARE

Saul told his son Jonathan and all his officials
that he planned to kill David.
    - I Samuel 19.1

Because David & Jonathan

touch. After the youth, carrying arrows back to town, has gone.
    In the field soft with shot bodies of birds.
In the field that is a kiss, text made real
    by rot, claw and wing, and maggots' mouths
glossing the white lines of feather and bone. They touch

and air leaches riches from milkweed, each pod a burst
    coinpurse, seeds like lambent metals spent and aloft. Touch
(youth gone, his quiver filled with feathers),
    and the father's body marks the field's edge, fear
a hard dirt road to town where skin's worn loose

    like cotton cloth. Touch : the Book's page's turned,
both were crying as they kissed each other, verse declaimed
    to a congregation, 1984, field made real in Alabama,
in a church where heat of day and red clay dust
    swarmed the windows, cut and stained glass where angels edited

the text of Heaven, church where the preacher's lips erased
    the men's skin-to-skin in the boy's — *my* — mind. His childhood
lost the ruin that is their kisses, text, field where two men
    are losing each other to the white page of day, watching grass knife up

ciphers in the light, small bodies of never-again feathered
    and easy with gore in the heat. *Once again Jonathan made David promise*
to love him in the text, enough only for the shallow kiss
    of the word "friend." Their names' necessary knives skimmed his skin,
childhood desire the sinewy scar that grew over the wound

    of their touches, his mind a book where the most someone could write
was : *better even than the love of women* : enough
    to love them like this, back-lit with the losses of history, to note
the way the preacher lip-synched, cinched lips
    that ask me still to name this kiss otherwise. Carrying arrows,

the youth — a boy himself — stops on the road back,
    wind loose in its slough of red dust, wind spreading bright seed

in a quick circumference, and the boy turns, text
   deepening in the light, two men losing the field to something

brighter, erasure, the boy's gaze taking it in, their body
   called love staked out in the grass against the historical
edge of the father's body.
   The boy I was knew the plot from here :
the field's blueprint suggests a bier

   for the beloved; the road delivers
his father's orders to march in a war
   he won't survive; and never was anyone so much a coward
as David now, silent even beneath the oath
   of kisses, among the grasses who make a pleasant measure of rot

and heat as they pitch song against themselves,
   this King who will sing so well of love only after his lover is dead.
The boy witnessed the preacher allow Jonathan to say

   The Lord will make sure that you and I,
and your descendents and mine, will forever keep
   the sacred promise we have made each other,

and he feared the preacher could make the Lord
   make sure of anything, say anything in that church
wearing the red cotton shroud of dust loose
   in summer air, in that stifled heaven where angels enumerated
the blessed on lists rich with editing,
   and the boy thought he knew already —

pressed hot on the pew between mother's thigh and father's elbow —
   how a secret skin's worn tight as summer behind the knees.

But he couldn't see this silence only begins

   the story, the long one the preacher made the Lord name
sinful, where two men lose themselves forever
   to something brighter in a field whose air bristles static
with the electricity of seed, where the only road out is death.

   Fear marked the beginning of the father's body in me :

there is no road out of the body they make in the field.

               for Jim Elledge

DANIEL NATHAN TERRY

I would hold you in my arms,

crazy preacher's-boy, until you see it's not a pillar of cloud
or a pillar of flame — just your head full of thunder
and the coming of a storm.
                              But how can I go back
thirty-four years and convince you that your skull is a hive
of madness as you pump the pedals of your little bike
through the neighborhood of the lost, bible tucked under
your arm like a loaf of good bread you meant to share?
                                                      How
can I dissuade you from banging on screen doors to warn
your neighbors that the end is coming, that the darkening
sky *like a sack of black feathers* proves everything the prophet said
is now on their doorstep?
                          You are seven years old, and so certain,
and you see it in your mind — horsemen of smoke and bones,
maggots in the skulls of those who will not be called, endless
lines of unraptured scarecrows ready to take the mark of the beast
for a crust of bread and a sip of black water.
                                              And you would
forgive them all if you were God — those who find it impossible
to worship love — the family that screams at each other
down the street, that drink whiskey a block away, even
the next-door neighbors who haven't saved their own son,
your best friend and the object of those shameful dreams
you've prayed to have lifted from the darkness inside you.
                                                          You
can see him, burning. And even if I could return to you, what right
have I to say that you are mistaken? That your head is simply full
of some long-dead man's angry ravings — a man who had
watched the love of his life crucified — when your small body hums
with the terrified bees
                        that have burrowed in beneath your eyes,
that have tunneled in through your ears, seeking sanctuary,
making honeyed prophecies, some three decades before
you will watch the honey bees vanish from clover and combs
like Jews from shops, from the flowers that once bloomed
beneath their hands in the gardens of 30s Berlin.
                                                  They're in my head.
Your head. Our heads are full of the missing. God,
if you ever walked among us, open our mouths. Make of our bodies a field
of flowers. Let Your dark second coming
be a storm of bees.

Because you read on the web

that the medusa of *Turritopsis nutricula* is an immortal
jellyfish — a tiny god no more than five millimeters long
and able to bypass death, to return from its adulthood
to its childhood after breeding or suffering
some other trauma —
                                you wonder if the eternal-life
that religions promise should be reserved for these little ghosts
with their red crosses of blood lodged in transparent bodies
that float above ninety arms so thin they are nearly invisible
to the human eye, but no less the arms of a hunter.
                                                And you wonder,
like a philosopher twirling five millimeters of an immortal stone
between his finger and thumb, if it would be a blessing to revert
back to your own childhood, to skip the coming losses of old age,
the winnowing of strength and love that is, as a human,
unavoidable.
                        And it is too simple to say that the part of you
who wants to die is the one who lights up a smoke, the one who once
had sex with strangers in strange bedrooms and against the filthy
back walls of bars. That years ago aimed his truck at the white trunk
of a giant, winter sycamore, floored the gas pedal
and took his hands off the wheel
                                thy will be done.
                                                And it's too simple
to say that the one who, this morning, envies the immortal medusa
is the one who is grateful that the truck lost traction and wheeled
safely into a hood-high snow-bank.
                                And it is wrong to say
that the one who would live forever is the one driving down
Independence Boulevard, hypnotized by the flowers of the flesh-
pink apricot trees as they drift into the black water of the roadside
ditch — each petal a half-shell that is also, before it sinks empty
into the mud, a fragile boat that could carry only the smallest of creatures,
if it were willing,
                        to the safety of the other shore.

TRUONG TRAN

the wake

the fluid
motion
of my aunt's
hand

the outstretched
paper fan
catching
tears

before
they could touch
his face
careful

she warns
no point
in holding
your father back

as if
with a fan
she clears
his path

ADDIE TSAI

Her lover blushed, and then she moved on. —

I knew the first time my volleyball coach's jagged fingernail caught on my jersey shorts as she tried to teach me a new serve. My mother's warning haunted my sleep — *what you're doing, it goes against God* — and so I gave him the backside of my black-haired head that night. For many nights. I relished in the freedom to give silence, my face a marvelous blank page. Someone told me once *step on a crack break your mama's back* so I stepped on as many cracks as I could find. I wanted to see her spine writhe beneath my pigeon toed sneakers, that tight lipped Korean mother glaring, my heart trapped between her claws. A hell most of you whities will never know. I fled. I sent my parents a letter to inform them that I would not, as they put it, *live a godly life*. It was the least I could do. My selfish desire. What pain it caused them. You know what they say. *Love the sin, hate the sinner*. My father came to me first. We met at a Jack in the Box, his face distorted in disgust, as though swarming in flies. We shared a large order of fries between us. I watched the little victim wilt from its death in grease, while my father taught me the rules of homosexuality within the family line, what happens in the army when there are no women hovering around their lined-up meat. *He lick my penis. You know, it feel good at first, but then I scream no, no, no. See, I could be gay, too. But. Hmm. That man, I talk to him. He married now, with family*. An emphatic nod. A twist of the twitches on his face. My mother, as always, comes last. She takes me to the beach. *If I born here, I probably be lesbian, too*. Closure is a kind of death. I stared through the ocean, watched it struggle against the sand.

AMY TUDOR

What We Love

I walk my old dog down a street called Holiday,
past trees whose white bark is trimmed with silver
in the light rain of early Spring. The dog's small heart
is failing and the vets said he shouldn't be out,
but if we walk slowly he can go four or five squares
of sidewalk, then I let him stop and rest.

He puts his nose up into the cool air, the wind ruffling
his black and white coat and the gray on his ears,
the wind smoothing over him. When he can't go
any further (halfway past that lovely ochre-colored house
in my neighborhood, the one that's half-hidden by linden
and guarded by an iron gate), I carry him against my chest.

One day a black lab stood at a driveway gate
and barked at us as we passed. My old dog
looked from beneath half-lidded eyes and didn't answer,
and finally the other dog's owner, an older man,
came out the screen door and called the dog to come back.
The dog rose from where he sat, a hind leg dragging
and his right front hitched as he moved toward the house.
I watched it go. The man looked at me holding
my old dog against my chest. The man smiled.
He raised a hand, half-greeting, half-regret.

I should say here that I know the rules I'm breaking.
I was told years ago that poets shouldn't waste
their time on trivial things like dying pets.
"It's been done, and done, and *done* to death,"
a friend once said. And it has, sure
as death's been done and done and *done* to death.

So I'll make a deal with you — forget
what I've said about my dog in my arms,
his nose in the air, the wind like hands. And forget
the man and his black lab that limped up
those brick back steps. I won't write about any of that.
I'll write a poem about what we love instead.

What we love is a night and a house
wreathed with linden, the dark kept outside

a circle of light over an iron gate. It's fine
as silver paper or the wind of early Spring.
What we love is a tree that grows outside our window
as we grow inside its panes, a small good thing
we bring home — or that follows us there — one day.
Then it's a friend that walks with us, gentle
and welcome as rain. It's what we call to us to come
when darkness is coming, and it's what tends us,
and what we tend. And finally it's what we carry
close against us, feeling blessed as we hold it
and joy for what it gives and has given,
for the comfort it's been through hard, heavy days,
forgiving every burden it's been, grateful
for even the grief we must carry when it's gone,
that soft, warm, impossible weight.

STEVE TURTELL

A Prayer

Sunday Morning: Gay Pride Day 2001.
I breakfast alone at the Café Colonial.

Rita waits on me; I read the Times,
glance out at quiet Houston St.

At 9 am, the café is still empty
Then in comes a tribe of teenage boys,

carrying books and notepads,
escorted by a plump man in gray.

His book has a frayed, twisted ribbon.
Ah, the cover is Bible Black.

They sit opposite me,
a religious group visiting Sin City.

I eat my omelet, homefries, toast.
Halfway through the Book Review

I glance up. One of the boys
is staring right at me. Sadness,

maybe even desire in his glance.
I recognize myself in him,

as he wonders about me.
He is handsome and shy.

And afraid. And alone.
Please God, don't let them

destroy him. Show him
he is loved and worthy.

Keep him from self-hatred.
Give him enough good fortune

to make him happy, enough
misfortune to make him wise.

Pears

We met over 40 years ago. Floating buttucky halves
  spooned into pastel fruit bowls, even drowned in
    Del Monte syrup, love at first taste. Your flesh

a luminous hue, hovering on the border of cream
  and August skies; your flavor pure as dreamed pleasure
    grazing my waking tongue, a melting sweetness

streaming down my throat; your name, a single syllable
  promising delight: pear, barely sound, mere parting of lips,
    and hint of breath, apple-green p, the sweetest

diphthong ea, all the air in the world, closed in rounded rr'd
  finality. A perfect word, reducing your rumpled, pinnacled
    self, to one gorgeous, Old English syllable: per.

Right now, six of you sit ripening on my window-sill.
  A sky-blue towel shields bottoms against further bruising
    from the wood even at birth you instinctively flee, hanging

off trees in swelling green-gold tears, yearning for earth,
  or growing to maturity in bottled, olive-green light, your dying
    breath suffusing aging liqueurs like the oldest I ever drank,

the summer I was 19, a century old brandy served in snifters
  the likes of which this working class boy had never seen.
    I tilted the giant crystal bowl; the fragrant liquid elongated

in mimicry of its remembered self and seeped into my mouth: a pear's
  ghost enveloped in flame lay down to rest on my tongue. We both
    were saved, at least for that night. Pear. Look of women I love

but don't lust after, I want to conjugate you: I pear, you pear,
  we pear. Like raspberries, Mozart and love, for me, sufficient proof
    of God's existence. I trust you. Lead me by the tongue to heaven.

MEGAN VOLPERT

Adults are children like weapons are tools

Uncle Saul had to pick me up from preschool and one day told me I was beginning to grow a monkey tail. The next week, he said it looked longer. I confess I did a shoulder check, but he said only grown ups could see it. Aunt Fran corroborated and I commenced freaking out. This is partly why it took me awhile to come out of the closet. Twenty years later, we were sitting shiva for my grandmother. On day three, I stuck a finger in Saul's back and told him he was beginning to grow a monkey tail. He had no idea what I was talking about.

Religion is in the mail

There have been a dozen bar mitzvahs, weddings and funerals. I have never set foot in a house of worship uninvited and never lived in a house with high ceilings. My wife will not get a tattoo because she wants to be buried in a Jewish cemetery. My mother-in-law plucked her eyebrows into oblivion and then tattooed them back on. She's also never been drunk, whereas I once drank two forties of King Cobra every night for seventy days. When I say I will be cremated because I am afraid of zombies, people laugh as if I am kidding, but the body is the temple.

A place without work is no heaven to me

Sometimes during orgasm I see the faces of dead friends. They are waving and smiling with laughter from up and across, happy I have checked in by flinging a moment of condensed purity over the wall between us. I believe they are working as much as I am, finishing business and settling their accounts. Glad as I am to see them, sometimes one of these faces disappears where I can't get it back again, and I celebrate that they have found enough peace to get recycled. Whatever the methods, a soul is the part of humanity that is a perpetual motion machine.

The Two of Wands

I remember how good a reading we got
when Katie talked me into her tarot cards
for once she was an expert
in control of our interview with destiny
ready to determine if her future was kissing me
when I drew the Ten of Cups
and seizing an obvious moment
the deck spilling as our knees met
our hands met our lips met

but after our bodies came apart
stuck to my back was the Nine of Swords
and I have not seen Katie in years

ARISA WHITE

dagger

My freedom was learned twice by fire. My lover's stove took over, every hair
brought to ash. I was later told, *Good thing you didn't breathe, the flame would
have found energy for more.*

In my dream the hellfire was not what my brother described. I dropped
chocolate from my s'mores onto the coals and no body cried. He said I would be
punished for my truths, be party to the woman who proved her devotion by
eating her lover's endometrial waste — is this what you want to do as a lesbian?

Sometimes his thoughts are poor, simple in their geometric shape; fits dogma in
his mouth like a woof and bark a testament he can't substantiate. It's choice; he
beats the bible instead of assist his heart in shaking off its necrotic crust.

Murder is not the point of my life, left to live in the cells of his correction, in the
least populated hours, dismissed of my caw.

We fly branch-tethered. My family thinks they know the cost of their heirlooms,
woven to make the suffering tight, their heads can't turn for fear of a salt-pillar's
life. We need to let angels in our doors, every creature needs stranger company
to know the nay and yea of its comportment, the topography and
unmentionables of its god.

Surprised I've become the self I long before consented to, maybe now they'll
see the river plainly in their faces, their smiles without the flood, the silt rich and
begging: *Here, my seed as natural as the sheath you put me in.*

MARVIN K. WHITE

Suite Jesus

I.

God of the FDA and of combination drugs. The one true Atripla and
Combivir God. The Epzicom of prayers. The first Trizivir and the
last Truvada. The Great Fuzeon, Lord of the Entry and Fusion
Inhibitors. Mother and Father Nucleoside and Non-Nucleoside
Reverse Transcriptase Inhibitors. My Rescriptor, my Sustiva God
and my Viramune God. The one they call Ziagen and the Trizivir of
Peace. The Epzicom Sample and The Videx Hope. My Emtriva
waking and my Epivir sleeping God. The bottle twister of my Zerit
and the sweet coating of my Viread. The deliverer of my Retrovir.
The God of opportunity in opportunistic infection. God of the Living
Rifadin. The True AmBisome shining. The Zithromax light. The Pill
Giver. The Most High Radiesse. My Biaxin keeper And the one
Whose Date Does Not Expire. My Liposomal God. The Mysterious
Dissolving one. The man they call Marinol of Oakland, Baraclude of
Atlanta, Procrit of New York, Etopophos of Jackson, Toposar of
Chicago and Diflucan of DC. The Elixir. The I AM. The Cytovene. I
AM. The Globulin. I AM. The Nydrazid. I AM. The Sporanox. I AM.
The Faithful Megace. The one who prescribes My Taxol,
Peginterferon, Alfa-2 god. The Holding It All Down God of my
Mycobutin and Serostim. Sweet, sweet, sweet Serostim. My
Bactrim and my Septra. My Main Man. My Depo-Testosterone.
The One on Trial. Agenerase-Reyataz-Prezista-Lexiva-Crixivan-Kaletra-
Viracept-Norvir-Fortovase-Invirase-Aptivus-Aptivus-Aptivus-Aptivus-
Aptivus-Aptivus-That's The One called Hope! The one who brought
hope! The Blood Giver and the Blood Taker. Oh my
Pneumocystis Carinii, Cytomegalo, Toxoplasmosis,
Cryptococcussporidiumdiosis, Meningitis, Enterocolitis,
Mycobacterium, Avium Complex, Tuberculosis, Bacillary-
Angiomatosis, Salmonella, Non-Hodgkin's Lymphoma, Retinitis
Kaposi Sarcoma, Progressive Multifocal Leukoencephalopathy
GOD! The God of my Morphologic Change. The God who is both
change and constant. The Lipodystrophy and Atrophy and Trophic
god. The God riding my Buffalo Hump. The Way Maker of
Cardiovascular Disease. The One Not Wasting this, my wasting.
The Saccharine God of my diabetes. The One higher than my high
cholesterol and my triglycerides. Oh my Dyslipidemias, Insulin
Resistance, Gynecomastia, Hyperlactatemia, Visceral Adiposity,
Hyperlipidemia, Infective Endocarditis, Myocardial Infarction,
Histoplasmosis God! Still GOD! The One who temples
headaches. The Fever Fanner, Fatigue Breaker, Rash Clearer and
Flu Shaker. Jehovah Jireh. Jehovah Rapha. Jehovah Nissi.

Jehovah Shalom. Jehovah Ra-ah. Jehovah Sidkenu. Jehovah
Shammad. Jehovah Elohim. Jehovah Sabaoth. El Elyon. El
Adonai. El Shaddai. El Olam. God of inches. He-she god.
Brister God. La Transformista, the Transgender God. The First and the
Fifteenth god. The Social Working God. The Clinic and the County
Hospital God. The Welfare God. The Long Line and the Long Wait
God. The Deep Breath before I break God. The
Ohmmmmmmmmm before I jump across this desk and down her
throat God. My Mother God. The God of ash. Our Midnight Cry
God. Our Helper. Our Ouch God. Hearing our inside God. God
working in the medicine. God working through the medicine. God
working of the medicine. God working around the medicine. God
working on the medicine. My ADAP way maker and always my
amen when aint no men. My amen. My amen. My amen.

II.

They have come to me before these spirit boys. I have pulled down
their pants. They have I Chinged me. Misread my misfortune as
calling. Spilled their tealeaves onto my belly. Asked for skin. A
poem. Muscle memory. I have rocked inside of them, scattering
their trick tarot deck onto floors. They conjure me. Juju they way
in my head. Bold. Lay cosmology down in front of me. "Right
now," they all say, "I got a word for you." I know how to get it out
of them. Say, "Heal me." Say, "Give me your gift." Say, "Jesus."
Say, "Yemeya." Say, "Buddha." It is my weakness to love these
boys. It is their curse to love me.

III.

Write down their names. Writing is magic. Is a grounding
thing. Connects floating stories to paper and earth. Write down
their names. The three that called you last night because they
were lonely or because somehow they thought that you could
help them understand their fear of greatness. Write down their
names. Write down the one that spoke of family, the one of
health and the other of dreams. Be where you supposed to be so
you can receive the calls that you supposed to receive. You the
go-to and the got-to-go-too. Hear yourself when you hear them
speak. Be spoken to. Be looked up and spoken down to. All of
it is good. You got wisdom on reserve. Save a plate for stragglers
and strangers and visitors and family and friends who come by
phone and foot with their weary tales or their victory stories.
You will not be undone. Pray they come. Be what you pray for.
Practice knowing the difference between people's reception and
perception of you. Show more gratitude. Even when you can't
think of nothing you thankful for. Go deeper. Try sleeping for
visions and not just for rest. And rising early. Sleep for a word.

Sleep to get your breath back. Sleep to get your inroads dug.
Visions coming. Remove any question from your hands as you
write, build, bake, move things, spin things. Remove yourself
from fights and battles, real and imagined. Release persecution.
You ain't no pressure cooker. Simmer down. Show up. Get to
where you supposed to be, then maybe, just maybe, somebody
will be inspired, comforted, guided, unburdened by seeing you
being there. Because of Sunday, Monday is.

IV.

Know cows layin' down mean mosquitoes bitin' more than
fish. Know this for years. Know to arrive as the river stop
slapping his shore of a wife. Know his swoll chest is a threat.
Know when its mouth is full of rock and foam spit that it's been
drinkin'. Know river don't know nothin' but go. Know to wait
to see what has refused to be carried back out, what spilled thing
will be too heavy or too sacred to be given up. Know after what
rain, beneath what tree, under what moon wait black worms fat
like babies on they backside. And know it come back home
twelve night or twelve high more faithful than anything or
anyone. Better than a man. Know how much time you got, how
much more than acting quick it will take. Know to dig the way
my mother taught me to, quieting the sand, sweeping it low like
pride-kept dirt floors, cupping it hand full after soaked handful,
packing it tight, like perfect brown sugar measure. It should not
fly; the hole must be deep. The hole must be wide. Know
dreamin' of fish mean somebody pregnant. Don't mean they
gon have or keep a baby, just mean they got fucked. Know to wait
at this broken place in this shore's skin for this day's water
returned, this day's ways dirty and dark and thick to come back
like somebody who know where they left they stuff do. It will. It
come back angry and fast, not to me but the way it has come its
entire life — home. Know to read tealeaves on second and third
pass, to take the sediment and the sentiment gathered and pour
slowly like too much sugar in daddy's coffee cup. And pour, the
way my mama taught me. Know you can always put something
in a man's drink to make him behave. Know displace and know
this place, the fins breaking water, what whisker with what tail.
Know to throw the small ones back. Ain't worth the bone to
choke on. Know bare hand can snatch these cats, these pike, this
perch, this drowning angel, this old woman river, not my
mother, know. To water I am worth coming home to.

V.

A meat offering needs rest. My body has been
cooking. Claims itself a Sabbath. I have a testimony.

In the name of our Barbra. In the name of our Aretha.
In the name of our Holy Sylvester. I am an awkward
preaching thing ascending the staircase. A pew of
partners in row search me for Adam's Apple, feet,
thickness, like I stole something from them. I am
here per my request-fervent hormones and effective
prayer, a reconstruction surgery, a voice to match my
given word.

Thumbing their loose dollars, they wait for my
showstopper moment, a fall from stiletto grace, a
crown of thorn wig unhinged from my stocking cap, an
old gospel record scratching into an already scratchy
throat. I am I am I am I am I am. I am the prayer
request, not the song. I will not false a falsetto
for you. This is not the moment to run, to see if my breath
holds, flim flam for my sin, for confetti drops, for tips.
My voice is still as deep as their fathers. They can
hear me calling them Junior. The men from single
mothers get it. Have seen the ventriloquist's act.
Have seen the voice of a man thrown out of a still speaking
woman.

On the railroad tracks in the backfields where we
gathered, tree dark and city dark different. In one
if you are chased you likely to hit a wall, meet your
end. In the other you are in Eden. Don't have to hide
to be hidden. This is our lip-synched prayer circle.
Heels dug into holy ground. If you chased you meet
your maker. The trees love us. Nymph and lymph
us. Alter us. Altar us. Watch us forage for a place,
identity, belonging, reconciliation of face and dress
and tucked dick direction and volition and off the
shoulder numbers over creased and pleated slacks,
agency and fitting rooms to try on the soundtrack that
our blockbusting bodies courageous to. There are
many who pass this way. There are some and hum
left here.

There is a Pentecost for me and this pump of drag
queens called me. These mine. This fan of flames
confounding and confusing. This lisp is a sign. It has
never been safe out there for black girls. It will surely
never be safe for black boys who turn black girls. We
are the thing hard to swallow. A deciphering to come.
A new cloud to witness. A new jawbone to be spoken
through and broken through.

CYRIL WONG

religion

My parents go to church every Sunday,
buoyed by that weightless certainty

they call faith. Atheist that I
claim to be, perhaps my faith in love

is its own religion, its variations
like movements in the longest piece

of orchestral music, a fear of loss
a leitmotif repeated throughout

our private histories. And maybe,
like god, love is an inaudible song

heard only by that third ear
pricking open inside our heads,

heard during the return of an urgent
embrace, an angel's quietly sung

bass note sending almost im-
perceptible vibrations through the air,

stirring alive those curtains on either
side of the night-hollowed window.

At this moment, I may almost begin
to decipher the unwritten score

underlying the here and now, coolly
dictating the tempo of those pages

of clouds turning over this house —
at first *piu lento*, then *adagio* —

or the timed pauses between each
breath of the man unawake beside me,

a blueprint behind the harmony
of our contrapuntal sighs in the dark.

god is our mother

1

God is our mother
and does not exist

without her children
who are leaving;

without her husband
who has already left

through the backdoor of their marriage
into a backyard of indifference.

We are the atheists,
who do not believe in her love.

Yet we hear about it
all the time.

2

Can we teach God to love us better?
Our mother still believes

all that she is doing
is to love. Maybe we have done

too little to persuade her
to listen more, oppress us less.

Maybe we gave up
too easily when our mother

never stopped trying.
Maybe we are the sinners too.

3

God is our mother
who creeps into our rooms at night

while we are sleeping to check
that we have not sneaked out of the house

to meet friends she despises
because they have no curfew.

God is waiting
at the window, resisting sleep

as it yanks with little hands
at the fraying hem of her consciousness,

stiff with worry
and a frustrated desire to scold.

When we come through the door,
we will see her, a taut figure

cut out from the dark, refusing
to be forgotten. She will say nothing.

We will apologise. She will
say nothing, but she will sigh.

We will turn from her as she walks
back to her room,

the nothing she will say
gathering in the air of the living

room like a sharp smell
that will not leave, seeping

deep into our clothes, our hair,
the smell of guilt

we will remember her by.

MARK WUNDERLICH

Coyote, with Mange

Oh, Unreadable One, why
have you done this to your dumb creature?
Why have you chosen to punish the coyote

rummaging for chicken bones in the dung heap,
shucked the fur from his tail
and fashioned it into a scabby cane?

Why have you denuded his face,
tufted it, so that when he turns he looks
like a slow child unhinging his face in a smile?

The coyote shambles, crow-hops, keeps his head low,
and without fur, his now visible pizzle
is a sad red protuberance,

his hind legs the backward image
of a bandy-legged grandfather, stripped.
Why have you unhoused this wretch

from his one aesthetic virtue,
taken from him that which kept him
from burning in the sun like a man?

Why have you pushed him from his world into mine,
stopped him there and turned his ear
toward my warning shout?

EMANUEL XAVIER

The Omega Has Been Postponed

Jesus has decided to hold the second Coming on another planet
to allow other life forms the opportunity of more interesting ways of killing him
while, down on Earth, the cult of Catholicism enjoys
the materialism of crucifixes
and awaits a forced apocalypse
assuring the fanfare of his arrival by claiming everything
from New Orleans to Haiti
as proof that he loves them and only them
Despite the fact he has not even called for over two thousand years
Perhaps someday, *fua!*, he will grace us with a visit
Until then, Earth remains the asshole of the universe

TOM YATES

Soham

I am Thomas.

But also, sometimes, Tom. I have been Lila and Maya, Kala and Kartikeya, Ananta, Ananda and Yama.

I am crushed blackberries, sage and trampled mud, the sleekness of the adder and a branch cut from the weeping ash. I am slices of apple and milk warmed in the sun. I am the crackle of rain on leaves and the slam of shutters thrown open by wind.

I know the spirit caught in the heart of the oak. I know the warmth of your chair and the view from the turn of the stairs. I know the raven's nest and the heart of the padlocked park, the taste of your ear and the mole on the nape of your neck. I know the clock by the fire and the spider behind the dresser.

I was there when the towers of Atlantis became home to fishes and sea-urchins. I was there when the pyramids were built and the Nile began to flow, when ash obscured the sun and the earth became the deep.

I have been a rat in the hold of a ship. I have been an antelope running through trees to the river, a white rabbit crouched by a mirror and a dragonfly perched on a bulrush. I have been a vein in a dead man's wrist, the shape of an osprey's wing and the shadow cast by a moth as it circles the light.

I hid the egg with veins of midnight-blue, whose world was a forest of spears, whose ending was light and a mud hut crammed with corpses. I took fire from the gods and gave it to man; I held up the sky and stole the golden apple; I brought myrrh to the feet of God and nailed him to the cross.

I have been a torch held to the roof of a wooden house.
I have been a mirror held to the face of a dying man.
I have been shadow. I have been laughter.

I am Thomas.

Meltwater

The lines that intersect across your palm
are paths between the ashram and the pool

where we swam in winter under banks of clay.
The day we went alone down thinning paths

where stones lay glistening between the roots,
your outline was a doorway into dusk,

your mouth a mine with veins of copper ore.
I knew the way, but followed as you hurried

across log bridges, through the briars and mud,
your sandals growing black. You didn't speak

after we left the pool where crimson leaves
floated in icy water and the snake

had left his rock to twine around the roots
of the hollow elm. I walked as if asleep,

following you through thickening lines of rain,
through clumps of oaks and maples, over streams

born from the storm and flowing to the pool.
You grew in silence as I grew in words,

climbing the path that led back to our cells,
to the echoing hall of fragrant smoke and marble.

Your face was flint and tinder washed with rain
when you glanced back below the temple door.

CRYSTAL YBARRA

Dear Pastor

for Pastor Brian A.

Dear Pastor,

You probably don't remember me or you never would have accepted my friend request on Facebook. I was 14 years old when we last spoke. But before we go any further, lets both take a second to acknowledge your role as an institutional and spiritual gatekeeper. You chose a life of great responsibility, morality and power. You hold yourself to a power that is said to be all powerful, all knowing, all mighty; everywhere at once. I know that for myself I never felt your God's love without doubt in my heart, but especially on that day we last spoke.

Dear Pastor,

Once upon a time a 14 year-old girl was lonely and lost when she walked into   your church just down the street from the house where she grew up. One day in church you made a remark about nobody in your congregation being homosexual . . . and you were proud of that. She was only 14 but she spoke up anyway because she wanted to believe but she knew she was queer. She asked to talk to you after service a week later and so you did. She repeated your remark   and told you that it wasn't true, she was queer. She told you how your comment made her feel invalidated, made her feel hurt. She went to your church for over a year. But you just sat there. And with a cold face you told her she wasn't a partof your congregation because she never spoke in tongues so she couldn't be baptized into your church. Therefore, the statement you made was accurate.

Dear Pastor,

A 14 year-old girl you once spoke to grew up, got wise and has a message for you. Thank you. You closed a gate to me that could have kept me ignorant forever. You could have embraced me and tried to comfort and care for and guide me, but you didn't. You shut me out from a God that is supposed to be "all loving." I don't know if your God exists, but I also don't know if there isn't something else out there, something my people believed in since the dawn of time. Long, long before your people came over on ships shoving your God down our throats with great force; stripping us of our Creator that made people like that 14 year-old girl Two-Spirited on purpose. Your people killed many of my people in the name of your "all loving" God. Your God was everywhere at once, guiding your people through the raping and killing of my people, who died for the chance to teach their children of our people's Creator.

Dear Pastor,

The thing about 14 year-old little girls is that they grow up. And some of them never stop searching for where they belong just because another white man tried to break another insignificant brown skinned girl.

Dear Pastor,

Will I go to your hell if I say, "Fuck you!"? You were not able to break me because the Creator my people believe in gave me two spirits to make me two times stronger, when, say, a Pastor doesn't tell the child he's talking to the real history of how his God told his people to kill her people and take them away from their Creator.

Dear Pastor,

When I am with a woman I know that there is nothing more natural in the world. Your people with their God may have taken away the chance for many of my people to ever get to know their Creator because you've shoved your God down our throats for so long and with such great force.

Dear Pastor,

You can't oppress me anymore. My spirits have risen and I am twice as whole and twice as perfect, twice as happy knowing that there could be a Creator out there who loves me twice as much as your God is capable of.

contributor BIOGRAPHIES

Franklin Abbott has been practicing psychotherapy for decades and is a graduate of Mercer University and the University of Georgia School of Social Work. He is the author of three anthologies about men and gender; *Boyhood: Growing Up Male: A Multicultural Anthology* (University of Wisconsin Press, 1998) is the most recent. His first book of poetry and memoir, *Mortal Love*, was published by RFD Press in 1999 and his most recent, *Pink Zinnia: Poems and Stories*, appeared in 2009. He is chairperson of the Atlanta Queer Literary Festival.

Kazim Ali has worked as a political organizer, lobbyist and yoga instructor. His books include three volumes of poetry, two novels, a collection of essays and a volume of journals on spiritual practice. *Water's Footfall*, his translation of work by Iranian poet Sohrab Sepehri, was published by Omnidawn in 2011. Founding Editor of Nightboat Books, he teaches in the Creative Writing and Comparative Literature programs at Oberlin College.

Shirlette Ammons is a poet, musician and director of an arts program for children. She is also vocalist / songwriter for the hip hop rock band, Mosadi Music. Her collections include *Matching Skin* (Carolina Wren Press, 2008) and *Stumphole Aunthology of Bakwoods Blood* (Big Drum Press, 2002). She is a Cave Canem Fellow and recipient of the Kathryn H. Wallace Award for Artists in Community Service and the Durham Arts Council and United Arts Council Emerging Artist Grant.

Chrissy Anderson-Zavala is a Xicana writer from Salinas, California. She studied and taught poetry in June Jordan's Poetry for the People at UC Berkeley and has worked as a teaching artist with WritersCorps and the Performing Arts Workshop. Currently the Co-Deputy Director of Streetside Stories in San Francisco, she is a recipient of the San Francisco Arts Commission's Cultural Equity Individual Artist Commissions (2009 and 2011).

Jeffrey Angles (translator of Atsusuke Tanaka) is an associate professor of Japanese and translation at Western Michigan University. He is the author of *Writing the Love of Boys: Origins of Bishōnen Culture in Japanese Modernist Literature* (University of Minnesota Press, 2011) and translator of *Forest of Eyes: Selected Poems of Tada Chimako* (University of California Press, 2010) and *Killing Kanoko: Selected Poems of Itō Hiromi* (Action Books, 2009).

Ari Banias lives in Brooklyn, New York, where he works with used books and curates queer readings. His work has appeared in *Salt Hill, Aufgabe, FIELD, Cincinnati Review* and elsewhere. He is the recipient of residencies at Headlands Center for the Arts, Caldera and a 2011-2012 writing fellowship at Fine Arts Work Center in Provincetown.

Ellen Bass's poetry books include *The Human Line* (Copper Canyon Press, 2007) and *Mules of Love* (BOA Editions, 2002). Her poems have been published in *The Atlantic, The Kenyon Review, American Poetry Review, The Sun, The New Republic* and many other journals. Her non-fiction books include *Free Your Mind: The Book for Gay, Lesbian and Bisexual Youth and Their Allies* (Harper Perennial, 1996) and *The Courage to Heal* (Harper & Row Publishers, 1988). She lives in Santa Cruz, California, and teaches in the MFA poetry program at Pacific University. (*ellenbass.com*)

Jeffery Beam's award-winning works include *Gospel Earth* (Skysill Press, 2010), *The Beautiful Tendons: Uncollected Queer Poems, 1969-2007* (White Crane Books, 2008), *Visions of Dame Kind* (The Jargon Society, Inc., 1995) and the CD *What We Have Lost* (Green Finch Press,

2002). On World AIDS Day 2008, composer Steven Serpa premiered *Heaven's Birds* based on three poems from *The Beautiful Tendons*. *MountSeaEden*, *Midwinter Fires* and *The Broken Flower* are forthcoming collections. He is poetry editor at *Oyster Boy Review* and librarian at UNC-Chapel Hill. He lives in Hillsborough, North Carolina, with his partner of 31 years, Stanley Finch. (*unc.edu/~jeffbeam/index.html*)

Robin Becker's six collections of poetry include *The Domain of Perfect Affection* (University of Pittsburgh, 2006), *The Horse Fair* (University of Pittsburgh, 2000), *All-American Girl* (University of Pittsburgh Press, 1996), winner of the 1996 Lambda Literary Award in Lesbian Poetry, and *Giacometti's Dog* (University of Pittsburgh Press, 1990). She teaches at Penn State University and serves as Contributing and Poetry Editor for *The Women's Review of Books*, where she also writes a column called "Field Notes" on the national poetry scene. During the 2010-2011 academic year, she served as the Penn State Laureate.

Dan Bellm is a poet and translator living in San Francisco. He has published three books of poetry, most recently, *Practice* (Sixteen Rivers Press, 2008), winner of a California Book Award. His work has appeared in *The American Poetry Review*, *Poetry*, *Ploughshares*, *The Threepenny Review*, *The Best American Spiritual Writing* (Houghton Mifflin, 2004) and *Word of Mouth: An Anthology of Gay American Poetry* (Talisman House, 2000). He teaches literary translation at Antioch University Los Angeles and at New York University.

Oliver Bendorf is an MFA candidate at the University of Wisconsin-Madison, where he holds the Renk Distinguished Graduate Fellowship in Poetry. His work has appeared or is forthcoming in *Sugar House Review*, *Drunken Boat*, *Blood Orange Review* and elsewhere. He holds the BA from the University of Iowa and was a 2010 Lambda Literary Fellow.

Ahimsa Timoteo Bodhrán is the author of *Antes y después del Bronx: Lenapehoking* (New American Press, 2012) and editor of an international queer Indigenous issue of *Yellow Medicine Review: A Journal of Indigenous Literature, Art, and Thought*. His work appears in over a hundred publications in Africa, the Américas, Asia, Australia, Europe and the Pacific. A Michigan State University PhD candidate, he is completing *Yerbabuena/Mala yerba, All My Roots Need Rain: mixed-blood poetry & prose*.

Moe Bowstern has worked on commercial fishing vessels on and off since 1986. In 1996 she began publishing her adventures in her zine, *Xtra Tuf*, and now performs annually at the Fisher Poets Gathering every February in Astoria, Oregon. She has appeared at the Seattle Folklife Festival, the Working Waterfront Festival in New Bedford, Massachusetts. and the Sea Music Festival in Mystic, Connecticut. (*moebowstern.com*)

Ana Božičević is a poet and translator. Her *Stars of the Night Commute* (Tarpaulin Sky Press, 2009) was a Lambda Literary Award in Poetry finalist. She is a PhD candidate in English and Program Manager at The Graduate Center, CUNY, where she helped found *Lost & Found: The CUNY Poetics Document Initiative* and the Annual Chapbook Festival. With Amy King, she co-edits the journal *esque*. (*anabozicevic.com*)

Elizabeth Bradfield is the author of *Approaching Ice* (Persea Books, 2010), which was a finalist for the James Laughlin Award from the Academy of American Poets, and *Interpretive Work* (Arkoi Books / Red Hen Press, 2008), which won the 2009 Audre Lorde Prize and was a finalist for a Lambda Literary Award. Editor-in-chief of Broadsided Press (*broadsidedpress.org*) and a former Stegner Fellow, she works as a naturalist and lives on Cape Cod. (*ebradfield.com*)

Jericho Brown worked as the speechwriter for the Mayor of New Orleans before receiving the PhD in Creative Writing and Literature from the University of Houston. The recipient of the Whiting Writers Award and fellowships from the National Endowment for the Arts and the Radcliffe Institute at Harvard University, Brown is an Assistant Professor at the University of San Diego. His first book, *PLEASE* (New Issues Poetry & Prose, 2008), won the American Book Award.

Nickole Brown's *Sister*, a novel-in-poems, was published by Red Hen in 2007. The title poem from her forthcoming collection, *A Book of Birds*, won AROHO's 2010 Orlando Prize. In 2009 she received an National Endowment for the Arts fellowship. She worked at Sarabande Books for ten years and, for the past four, at Arktoi Books and the Marie Alexander Series. Currently, she teaches at Murray State and the University of Arkansas at Little Rock.

Regie Cabico is a spoken word theater artist and poetry slam pioneer. He took top prizes in the 1993, 1994 and 1997 National Poetry Slams and is a former Nuyorican Poets Cafe Grand Slam Champion. His work appears in over 30 anthologies including *Spoken Word Revolution* (SourceBooks Media Fusion, 2005), *The Outlaw Bible of American Poetry* (Basic Books, 1999) and *Aloud: Voices from the Nuyorican Poets Cafe* (Holt Paperbacks, 1994). He appeared on two seasons of HBO's Def Poetry Jam and performs throughout North America and England.

Michelle Cahill wrote *Ophelia in Harlem* (Kilmog Press, 2010) and *The Accidental Cage* (Interactive Press, 2006), shortlisted in the Judith Wright Prize, and edited *Poetry Without Borders* (Picaro Press, 2008). She was highly commended in the Blake Poetry Prize and won both the Val Vallis Award and the Inverawe Poetry Award. *Vishvarupa* (5 Islands Press, 2011) is her latest collection. She is a fellow at Hawthornden Castle in 2011 and is co-editing the *Puncher and Wattmann Anthology of Contemporary Asian Australian Poetry*.

Rafael Campo is the author of *Diva* (Duke University Press, 1999), *What the Body Told* (Duke University Press, 1996), which won a Lambda Literary Award for Poetry, *The Poetry of Healing: A Doctor's Education in Empathy, Identity, and Desire* (W.W. Norton, 1997), a collection of essays now available in paperback under the title *The Desire to Heal*, which also won a Lambda Literary Award for memoir, and *The Other Man Was Me* (Arte Público Press, 1994), which won the 1993 National Poetry Series Award. He is the Director of the Office of Multicultural Affairs at Beth Israel Deaconess Medical Center.

Ching-In Chen is the author of *The Heart's Traffic* (Arktoi Books / Red Hen Press, 2009). A Kundiman and Lambda Fellow, she is part of the Macondo and Voices of Our Nations Arts Foundation writing communities. Co-editor of *The Revolution Starts At Home: Confronting Intimate Violence Within Activist Communities* (South End Press, 2011), she has been awarded residencies at Soul Mountain Retreat, Vermont Studio Center, Paden Institute, Virginia Center for the Creative Arts and Millay Colony. (*chinginchen.com*)

Seung-Ja Choe (최승자), born in 1952, majored in German literature at Goryeo University. In 1979 she published her first poems in the quarterly journal *Munhakgwa Jiseong* (Literature and Intellect). Early poetry collections include *Love in This Age* (1981), *Fun Diary* (1984), *House of Memories* (1989) and *Green is My Grave* (1993), all published by Munhakgwa Jiseong Publishers.

Maya Chowdhry is a poet, playwright and inTer-aCtive artist. Her work is published in *The Seamstress and the Global Garment* (Crocus Press, 2009), *Healing Strategies for Women at War: Seven Black Women Poets* (Crocus Press, 1999) and in other anthologies and magazines such as

Ambit. She won the *Cardiff International Poetry Competition* and her poetry has travelled via film, audio and web. Recently, she exhibited a haiku sewn in cress. (*mayachowdhry.net*)

James Cihlar is the author of *Metaphysical Bailout* (Pudding House Press, 2010) and *Undoing* (Little Pear Press, 2008). His writing appears in *The American Poetry Review, Prairie Schooner, The Awl, Lambda Literary Review, Cold Mountain Review, Smartish Pace, Mary, Rhino* and *Forklift, Ohio*. The Fiction / Nonfiction Editor for Etruscan Press, he teaches at the University of Minnesota in Minneapolis and Macalester College in St. Paul.

Andrea Cohen is the author of the poetry collections *Kentucky Derby* (Salmon Poetry, 2011), *Long Division* (Salmon Poetry, 2009) and *The Cartographer's Vacation* (Owl Creek Press, 1999). She directs the Blacksmith House Poetry Series in Cambridge, Massachusetts. (*andreacohen.org*)

Steven Cordova's first full-length volume of poems, *Long Distance*, appeared in 2010 from Bilingual Review Press. His work has appeared in many journals and anthologies, and forthcoming are a short story in *Ambientes: New Queer Latino Fiction* (University of Wisconsin Press) and an essay in *The Other Latino: Writing Against a Singular Identity* (University of Arizona Press). He lives in Brooklyn, New York.

Edward DeBonis's poetry has appeared in numerous publications including *Bottomfish, Hawaii Review* and *Sanctified: An Anthology of Poetry By LGBT Christians* (Justin R. Cannon, 2008). His first full-length book of poetry, *Homonym*, was published by GLB Publishers in 2002 (*homonym.net*). He and his husband of seventeen years, Vincent, live in New York City. *Saints and Sinners*, a full-length feature documentary of their Catholic wedding, was produced by Avatar Films (2003), selected for inclusion in the Human Rights Watch Traveling Film Festival and appeared on Logo TV.

Neil de la Flor's publications include *Sinead O'Connor and Her Coat of a Thousand Bluebirds* (Firewheel Editions, 2011), co-authored with Maureen Seaton and winner of the Sentence Book Award; *Almost Dorothy* (Marsh Hawk Press, 2010), winner of the Marsh Hawk Press Poetry Prize and *Facial Geometry* (NeoPepper Press, 2006), co-authored with Maureen Seaton and Kristine Snodgrass. His work, both solo and collaborative, appeared in *Hayden's Ferry Review, Barrow Street, TriQuarterly Review, Pank, Prairie Schooner, Indiana Review* and *Court Green*, among others. He teaches writing and literature and writes for the Knight Arts and Art Burst Miami. (*neildelaflor.com*)

Joseph Delgado was born and raised in Albuquerque, New Mexico, and is the author of the self-published poetry collection *Buzzard Songs*. He has poems forthcoming in *Trajectory, Santa Fe Literary Review* and *Joto: An Anthology of Queer Chicano Poetry* (Korima Press). He currently resides in Mohave Valley, Arizona, with his life partner David.

Cheryl Dumesnil, winner of the 2008 Agnes Lynch Starrett Poetry Prize, is the author of *In Praise of Falling* (University of Pittsburgh Press, 2009), editor of *Hitched! Wedding Stories from San Francisco City Hall* (Da Capo Press, 2005) and co-editor, with Kim Addonizio, of *Dorothy Parker's Elbow: Tattoos on Writers, Writers on Tattoos* (Grand Central Publishing, 2002).

Blas Falconer is the author of *The Foundling Wheel* (Four Way Books, forthcoming) and *A Question of Gravity and Light* (University of Arizona Press, 2007). He is a co-editor of *Mentor and Muse: Essays from Poets to Poets* (Southern Illinois University Press, 2010) and *The Other Latino: Writing Against a Singular Identity* (University of Arizona Press, forthcoming). The recipient of an National Endowment for the Arts Fellowship and the Maureen Egen Writers Exchange, he coordinates creative writing at Austin Peay State University.

Danielle Morgan Feris is a White, Jewish, Queer, third-generation New Yorker. She is the Director of Hand in Hand (*domesticemployers.org*), which organizes domestic employers and their families in support of just workplaces for domestic workers. A community organizer for over a decade, she works toward transformative justice, in particular, alongside workers, immigrant communities and in solidarity with Palestine. She has a Jewish practice and is a member of a multi-racial Queer writing group called Agent 409.

John Frazier has published poetry and nonfiction in *The New Republic*, *The Gay and Lesbian Review Worldwide*, *The Antioch Review*, *The Massachusetts Review*, *Presence Africaine* and many other journals and anthologies. He writes sonnets and also paints large-scale canvases using sonnets. He has been a MacDowell Fellow and received other distinctions for his work. He lives and works in the San Francisco Bay Area.

J. Neil C. Garcia teaches creative writing and comparative literature at the University of the Philippines, Diliman, where he serves as a fellow for poetry in the Institute of Creative Writing. Co-editor of the famous *Ladlad* series of Philippine gay writing, he is the author of numerous poetry collections and works in literary and cultural criticism.

RJ Gibson's work has appeared in *Court Green*, *OCHO* and *Knockout*. He holds the MFA from the Program for Writers at Warren Wilson College. In 2008 he was a Poetry Fellow for Lambda Literary Foundation's New and Emerging Writers' Retreat. His chapbook, *Scavenge*, was a winner of the 2009 Robin Becker Competition. He lives and works in West Virginia.

Brent Goodman's fourth collection of poetry, *Far From Sudden*, is forthcoming from Black Lawrence Press. His most recent book, *The Brother Swimming Beneath Me* (Black Lawrence Press, 2009), was a finalist for both a Lambda Literary Award and a Thom Gunn Award. His chapbooks also include *Trees Are the Slowest Rivers* and *Wrong Horoscope*, winner of the Frank O'Hara Award. He lives in Rhinelander, Wisconsin, with his partner of 20 years.

Benjamin S. Grossberg teaches at The University of Hartford. His books are *Sweet Core Orchard* (University of Tampa, 2009), winner of the 2008 Tampa Review Prize and a Lambda Literary Award, and *Underwater Lengths in a Single Breath* (Ashland Poetry Press, 2007). His poems have recently appeared in *New England Review*, *North American Review* and *Missouri Review,* and are forthcoming in *Ninth Letter* and *The Best American Poetry* (Scribner, 2011).

Jeremy Halinen co-edits *Knockout Literary Magazine* (*knockoutlit.org*). *What Other Choice*, his first full-length collection of poems, won the 2010 Exquisite Disarray First Book Poetry Contest and is available online at *alibris.com*. His poems have also appeared in *Best Gay Poetry 2008* (Lethe Press), *Crab Creek Review*, the *Los Angeles Review*, *Poet Lore*, *Sentence* and elsewhere. He resides in Seattle.

Robert Hamberger's poetry has been broadcast on BBC Radio 4 and featured on the *Guardian Poem of the Week* website. He was awarded a Hawthornden Fellowship and shortlisted for the Forward prize. His full-length collections are *Torso* (Redbeck Press, 2007), *The Smug Bridegroom* (Five Leaves, 2002) and *Warpaint Angel* (Blackwater, 1997). In 2006 he was first prize-winner in *Chroma*'s first International Queer Writing Competition. He lives in Brighton, England.

Forrest Hamer is the author of *Rift* (Four Way Books, 2007), *Middle Ear* (Roundhouse, 2000), winner of the Northern California Book Award, and *Call and Response* (Alice James, 1995), winner of the Beatrice Hawley Award. His work appears in *The Best American Poetry* (1994, 2000, 2007). He has received fellowships from the California Arts Council and the Bread Loaf Writers Conference and has taught on the poetry faculty of the Callaloo Creative Writing Workshops.

Reginald Harris is the author of *10 Tongues: Poems* (Three Conditions Press, 2002). His work has appeared in a variety of publications including *African-American Review, MELUS Journal, Smartish Pace* and *Sou'wester,* and the anthologies *Best Gay Poetry 2008* (Lethe Press), *Gathering Ground: A Reader Celebrating Cave Canem's First Decade* (University of Michigan, 2006) and *The Ringing Ear: Black Poets Lean South (A Cave Canem Anthology)* (University of Georgia, Press, 2007). He is Poetry in the Branches Coordinator for Poets House.

Jen Hofer is a poet, translator, interpreter, teacher, knitter, book-maker, public letter-writer and urban cyclist. Her recent and forthcoming poem sequences and translations are available through a range of autonomous small presses including: Atelos, Counterpath Press, Dusie Books, Kenning Editions, Les Figues Press, Palm Press and Subpress. She also writes letters for people in public spaces at her escritorio público and makes tiny books by hand at her kitchen table in Cypress Park, Los Angeles.

Fanny Howe's latest book of poems is *Come and See* (Graywolf Press, 2011). Her other most recent books are *The Winter Sun: Notes on a Vocation* (Graywolf Press, 2009), a book of essays; and *What Did I Do Wrong?* (Flood Editions, 2009), a fable.

Azwan Ismail is a poet and writer from Malaysia whose work has appeared in local anthologies. He is the co-editor of *Orang Macam Kita* (Matahari Books, 2010), the first Malaysian LGBT anthology in Malay, and is now working on his first novel, *Disko*. Because of his courageous and controversial *It Gets Better* video, he was listed among the top 10 "gay rights heroes" of 2010 by Change.org. He lives in Kuala Lumpur, Malaysia.

Maria Jastrzębska was born in Warsaw, Poland, and came to the UK as a child. Her recent collections include *Everyday Angels* (Waterloo Press, 2009), *I'll Be Back Before You Know It* (Pighog Press, 2009) and *Syrena* (Redbeck Press, 2004). Her co-translation of Slovenian poet Iztok Osojnik's work is forthcoming from Pighog Press. Winner of Off_Press International Competition 2009, her work appeared in *Anthologia*. She has co-edited numerous anthologies including *Different and Beautiful* (Allsorts Youth Project, 2010) and *Whoosh! Queer Writing South Anthology* (Pighog, 2008). (*south-pole.co.uk*)

Joe Jiménez lives in San Antonio, Texas. His work has appeared in *Mariposas: New Queer Latino Poetry* (Floricanto Press, 2008), *Borderlands Texas Poetry Review* and is forthcoming in *Saltwater Quarterly, phati'tude Literary Magazine* and *Caper Literary Journal*. The short film "El Abuelo [1983]," commissioned as part of London's 2008 Fashion in Film Festival, is based on his affinity for ironing.

Irfan Kasban, a multi-disciplinary artist trained in dance, music and theatre, is an award-winning playwright based in Singapore. His plays include *CLASSIFIED: Projek Congkak, Genap 40, We Live in a Box* and *W.C.* He freelances as a director, lighting designer, actor and arts educator, and his works primarily consider language, fate and faith, drawing from inner resentment and hope.

Maya Khosla received the Dorothy Brunsman Poetry Prize for her first full-length poetry collection, *Keel Bone* (Bear Star Press, 2003). Her poetry has been featured in the anthologies *Fog & Woodsmoke: Behind the Image* (Lost Hills Books, 2011) and *Water: Culture, Politics and Management* (India International Centre, 2010), and in journals such as *Rhino, Poem* and *Prairie Schooner*. She has received awards from Poets and Writers, Inc., Ludwig Vogelstein Foundation, *Americas Review* and *Byline Magazine* and residencies from the Headlands Center for the Arts and Hedgebrook.

Jee Leong Koh is the author of three books of poems including *Seven Studies for a Self Portrait* (Bench Press, 2011). His poetry has appeared in *Best Gay Poetry 2008* (Lethe Press) and *Best New Poets* (University of Virginia Press, 2007). Born and raised in Singapore, he now lives in New York City and blogs at *Song of a Reformed Headhunter*.

Paula Kolek recently graduated from the University of Miami's MFA program. Her poems have appeared or are forthcoming in *Cake, New Letters, Otoliths, Wicked Alice, Almost Dorothy* and *Ditch*, among others. Her monologue was presented in The Krane's production of *Monologues Lingus* and her artwork published in *Fickle Muses*.

Keetje Kuipers earned the BA at Swarthmore College and the MFA at the University of Oregon. She was the Margery Davis Boyden Wilderness Writing Resident in 2007 and a Stegner Fellow at Stanford University (2009-2011). Her book, *Beautiful in the Mouth*, won the A. Poulin, Jr. Poetry Prize and was published by BOA Editions in 2010. She is now the Emerging Writer Lecturer at Gettysburg College.

Rickey Laurentiis was born and raised in New Orleans. His manuscript, *One Country*, received an honorable mention for the 2010 Benjamin Saltman Poetry Award. Other honors include first- and third-runner up in the 2009 International Reginald Shepherd Memorial Poetry Prize. The recipient of fellowships from the Cave Canem Foundation and the Atlantic Center for the Arts, his poetry has appeared or is forthcoming in several literary journals including *Indiana Review, jubilat, Knockout Literary Magazine* and *Vinyl*.

Joseph O. Legaspi is the author of *Imago* (CavanKerry Press, 2007). Recent poems appeared or are forthcoming in *From the Fishouse, jubilat, The Spoon River Poetry Review, Smartish Pace, PEN International* and *The Normal School*. A Queens, New York, resident, he co-founded Kundiman (*kundiman.org*), a non-profit organization serving Asian American poets. (*josepholegaspi.com*)

R. Zamora Linmark was born in Manila and educated in Honolulu. He is the author of two novels, *Rolling the R's* (Kaya / Muae, 1997) and its sequel *Leche* (Coffee House Press, 2011), and three collections of poetry from Hanging Loose Press: *Drive By Vigils* (forthcoming), *The Evolution of a Sigh* (2008) and *Prime Time Apparitions* (2005). He taught at the University of Hawaii and University of Miami. He currently resides in Honolulu and Manila.

Timothy Liu is the author of *Bending the Mind Around the Dream's Blown Fuse* (Talisman House, 2009), *Polytheogamy* (Saturnalia, 2009), *For Dust Thou Art* (Southern Illinois University Press, 2005), *Of Thee I Sing* (University of Georgia, 2004), selected by Publishers Weekly as a 2004 Book of the Year, *Hard Evidence* (Talisman House, 2001), *Say Goodnight* (Copper Canyon Press, 1998), *Burnt Offerings* (Copper Canyon Press,1995) and *Vox Angelica* (Alice James Books, 1992), which won the Poetry Society of America's Norma Farber First Book Award. He has also edited *Word of Mouth: An Anthology of Gay American Poetry*, (Talisman House, 2000).

Raymond Luczak is the author and editor of more than ten books including *Road Work Ahead: Poems* (Sibling Rivalry Press, 2011), *Mute: Poems* (A Midsummer Night's Press, 2010), and *Assembly Required: Notes from a Deaf Gay Life* (RID Press, 2009). His novel *Men with Their Hands* (Queer Mojo, 2009) won first place in the Project: QueerLit 2006 Contest. A filmmaker and playwright, he lives in Minneapolis, Minnesota. (*raymondluczak.com*)

Ed Madden is an associate professor of English at the University of South Carolina and the author of three collections of poetry: *Prodigal: Variations* (Lethe Press, 2011), *Signals* (University of South Carolina, 2008), winner of the 2007 South Carolina Poetry Book Prize, and *Nest*, forthcoming from Salmon Poetry. His work has appeared in *Best New Poets* (University of Virginia Press, 2007) and *The Book of Irish American Poetry from the 18th Century to the Present* (University of Notre Dame Press, 2007).

Maitreyabandhu lives and works in the London Buddhist Centre and has been ordained into the Triratna Buddhist Order for 20 years. He has won a number of prizes for his writing including the Keats-Shelley Prize, The Basil Bunting Award, the Geoffrey Dearmer Prize, First Prize in the 2009 New Writer Prose and Poetry Competition and the 2010 Ledbury Poetry Festival Competition. His books include *Life with Full Attention: A Practical Course in Mindfulness* (Windhorse Publications, 2011) and *Thicker than Blood: Friendship on the Buddhist Path* (Windhorse Publications, 2001).

Jeff Mann, winner of the Lambda Literary Award, has published three poetry chapbooks, three books of poetry, two collections of personal essays, a collection of memoir and poetry and a volume of short fiction. He teaches creative writing at Virginia Tech in Blacksburg, Virginia.

Sophie Mayer is a writer, editor and educator, based in London, UK. She is the author of two collections, *The Private Parts of Girls* (Salt, 2011) and *Her Various Scalpels* (Shearsman, 2009) and one critical text, *The Cinema of Sally Potter: A Politics of Love* (Wallflower, 2009). She is a Commissioning Editor at LGBTQ arts magazine *Chroma: A Queer Literary Journal* (*chromajournal.co.uk*). (*sophiemayer.net*)

Jill McDonough's first book of poems, *Habeas Corpus*, was published by Salt in 2008 and she has work forthcoming in *The Best American Poetry* (Scribner, 2011). The recipient of the Pushcart Prize and fellowships from the National Endowment for the Arts, the Fine Arts Work Center, the New York Public Library, the Library of Congress and the Stanford Stegner Fellowship Program, she has taught incarcerated college students through Boston University's Prison Education program since 1999.

John Medeiros' work has appeared in *Christopher Street, Evergreen Chronicles, Midway Journal, Sport Literate, Water-Stone Review, Gulf Coast, Willow Springs, Other Words: A Writer's Reader* (Kendall / Hunt, 2009), *Gents, Badboys and Barbarians* (Alyson Books, 1995) and many other publications. He is the recipient of two Minnesota State Arts Board grants and *Gulf Coast's* First Place Nonfiction Award. His work was a Notable Essay in *The Best American Essays* (Mariner Books, 2006). (*jmedeiros.net*)

Jay Michaelson is the author of *God vs. Gay? The Religious Case for Equality* (Beacon Press, 2011), as well as three books and 200 articles on the intersections of religion, spirituality, sexuality and law. His decade of advocacy for LGBT people in religious communities has been featured in *The New York Times*, NPR and CNN. He has taught at Yale, Boston University Law School, City College and in communities around the country. (*jaymichaelson.net*)

Dante Micheaux is the author of *Amorous Shepherd* (Sheep Meadow Press, 2010). His poems and translations have appeared in *The American Poetry Review, Bloom, Callaloo, Gathering Ground: A Reader Celebrating Cave Canem's First Decade* (University of Michigan, 2006) *and Rattapallax*, among other journals and anthologies. His honors include a prize in poetry from the Vera List Center for Art & Politics, the Oscar Wilde Award and fellowships from Cave Canem Foundation and The New York Times Foundation. He resides in London and New York City.

Susan L. Miller teaches Creative and Expository Writing at Rutgers University in New Brunswick, New Jersey. She serves as an LGBTQQIA liaison for students and helps to coordinate an LGBT reading series at Writers House. Her poetry has appeared in *Iowa Review, Meridian, Calyx, Commonweal, The Sewanee Theological Review* and *Los Angeles Review*, among others, and has twice won a Dorothy Sargent Rosenberg Prize. She lives in Brooklyn, New York.

Kamilah Aisha Moon's work has appeared or is forthcoming in several journals and anthologies including *Harvard Review, jubilat, Sou'wester, Oxford American, Gathering Ground: A Reader Celebrating Cave Canem's First Decade* (University of Michigan, 2006), *Callaloo* and *Bloom*. A featured poet in conferences and venues around the country, she has received fellowships from Cave Canem, the Prague Summer Writing Institute, the Fine Arts Work Center in Provincetown and The Vermont Studio Center. She received the MFA in Creative Writing from Sarah Lawrence College. (*kamilahaishamoon.org*)

James Najarian grew up on a farm in northern Berks Country, Pennsylvania. He teaches nineteenth-century poetry and prose at Boston College, where he also edits the scholarly journal *Religion and the Arts*. He published the critical work *Victorian Keats: Masculinity, Sexuality, and Desire* with Palgrave Macmillan in 2002. His poetry has appeared in journals including *Christianity and Literature, Primary Point, Tar River Poetry, West Branch* and *White Crane*.

Angelo Nikolopoulos is a graduate of NYU's creative writing program and the recipient of the 2011 "Discovery" / Boston Review Poetry Prize. His poetry has appeared in *The Awl, Boston Review, Boxcar Poetry Review, Gay and Lesbian Review, Los Angeles Review, Meridian, Mudfish* and elsewhere. He hosts The White Swallow Reading Series in Manhattan's West Village.

Shahril Nizam (translator of Azwan Ismail) is a painter, graphic designer and writer. He studied fine art at the Kuala Lumpur College of Art and the University of Melbourne, Australia. His paintings have been exhibited in Malaysia, Australia and Indonesia and he is the author of *If Only*, a book of poems and illustrations (Gores Press, 2007).

Mendi Lewis Obadike is the author of *Armor and Flesh* (Lotus Press, 2004) and forthcoming books with Keith Obadike: *Big House / Disclosure* and *Four Electric Ghosts*. Albums (also with Keith) include *The Sour Thunder, an Internet Opera* and *Crosstalk: American Speech Music*. She has received awards from Franklin Furnace, Cave Canem and NYFA. She is a poetry editor at *Fence Magazine*, an artist-in-residence at the Tribeca Performing Arts Center and an Assistant Professor at Pratt Institute.

G. E. Patterson is the author of *To & From* (Ahsahta Press, 2008) and *Tug* (Graywolf Press, 1999) and two chapbooks. Among other awards, his writing has received recognition from the Minnesota State Arts Board and New York's Fund for Poetry.

Christopher Phelps studied physics and philosophy at MIT. He now works in a small acrylic sculpture workshop. His poems appear in *FIELD*, *The Gay & Lesbian Review*, *The New Republic* and *Pank*, and are forthcoming in *The Awl*, *Boston Review* and *New York Quarterly*. He occasionally writes for *thethe.com*. (*christopher-phelps.com*)

Carl Phillips is the author of eleven books of poems, most recently *Double Shadow* (Farrar, Straus and Giroux, 2011) and *Speak Low* (2009). He teaches at Washington University in St. Louis.

Olumide Popoola, a London-based Nigerian-German writer, performer and guest-lecturer, presents internationally, often collaborating with musicians or other artists. She holds the BSc in Ayurvedic Medicine, the MA in Creative Writing and is currently a PhD candidate in Creative Writing at the University of East London. In 2004 she was awarded the May Ayim Award (Poetry), the first Black International Literature Award in Germany. Her novella *this is not about sadness* was published in 2010 by Unrast Verlag. (*olumidepopoola.com*)

D. A. Powell's books include *Chronic* (Graywolf Press, 2009) and *Cocktails* (Graywolf Press, 2004), both finalists for the National Book Critics Circle Award in Poetry. His honors and awards include fellowships from the National Endowment for the Arts, the James Michener Foundation, the California Book Award and the Kingsley Tufts Poetry Prize. He has taught at Harvard, Columbia, University of Iowa and Davidson College.

Katy Price was born in 1974 and lives in London, UK. Her poems have appeared in *Seam* and *Blackbox Manifold*, and her short story "Not at the Bovine Sex Club on Queen West" featured in *Chroma: A Queer Literary Journal*. She teaches English and Creative Writing at Anglia Ruskin University, Cambridge. (*katyprice.wordpress.com*)

Ruben Quesada is a PhD candidate at Texas Tech University. He is the author of *Next Extinct Mammal* (Greenhouse Review Press, 2011) and his poetry, reviews and translations have appeared in *Rattle*, *Stand Magazine*, *Southern California Review*, *Boxcar Poetry Review* and *Third Coast*. He has been a fellow at Squaw Valley Community of Writers, Lambda Literary Foundation Writer's Retreat, Vermont Studio Center, Santa Fe Art Institute and Napa Valley Writers' Conference.

Amir Rabiyah lives in Oakland, California. He received the BA in Women's Studies from Portland State University and the MFA in Writing and Consciousness from the New College of California. He has been published in *Mizna*, *Tea Party Magazine*, the Kearny Street Workshop's anthology *I Saw My Ex at a Party*, *Left Turn Magazine* and *Gender Outlaws: The Next Generation* (Seal Press, 2010). He was a finalist in *Cutthroat Magazine's* 2008 Joy Harjo Poetry Contest. (*amirrabiyah.com*)

Bushra Rehman is co-editor of *Colonize This! Young Women of Color on Today's Feminism* (Seal Press, 2002) and author of the poetry collection *Marianna's Beauty Salon* (Vagabond Press, 2001). Her work has appeared in *Crab Orchard Review*, *Sepia Mutiny*, *Color Lines*, *Mizna*, *Curve* and *SAMAR* and been featured in *The New York Times*, *India Currents*, *NY Newsday*, on BBC Radio 4, KPFA and the Brian Lehrer Show.

William Reichard is the author of four collections of poetry including *Sin Eater* (Mid-List Press, 2010) and editor of *American Tensions: Literature of Identity and the Search for Social Justice* (New Village Press, 2011).

Steven Riel is the author of three chapbooks of poetry, most recently, *Postcard from P-town* (Seven Kitchens Press, 2009), runner-up for the inaugural Robin Becker Chapbook Prize. In 2005 Christopher Bursk named him the Robert Fraser Distinguished Visiting Poet at Bucks County Community College. His poems have appeared in anthologies and numerous periodicals including *The Minnesota Review*. He received the MFA in Poetry from New England College.

Joseph Ross is a poet and teacher in Washington, D.C. His poems appear in many journals and anthologies including *Poetic Voices Without Borders 1* and *2* (Gival Press, 2005 and 2009), *Drumvoices Revue, Poet Lore, Tidal Basin Review, Beltway Poetry Quarterly* and *Full Moon on K Street*. In 2007 he co-edited *Cut Loose the Body: An Anthology of Poems on Torture and Fernando Botero's Abu Ghraib*. (*JosephRoss.net*)

Roberto F. Santiago received the BA from Sarah Lawrence College and currently teaches English Composition while completing the MFA at Rutgers University. His poetry has been published in *Me No Habla With Acento: Contemporary Latino Poetry* (El Museo / Rebel Satori Press, 2011), *-gape-seed-* (Uphook Press, 2011), *The Best of PANIC: En Vivo From the East Village!* (Rebel Satori Press, 2010) and *Dark Phrases: 20th Anniversary Edition* (Sarah Lawrence College, 2010). He lives in New York City.

Jason Schneiderman is the author of *Striking Surface* (Ashland Poetry, 2009), winner of the Richard Snyder Prize, and *Sublimation Point* (Four Way Books, 2004). His poetry and essays have appeared in numerous journals and anthologies including *American Poetry Review, The Best American Poetry* (Scribner, 2005), *Poetry London, The Penguin Book of the Sonnet* (2001) and *Tin House*. He has received fellowships from Yaddo, The Fine Arts Work Center and The Bread Loaf Writers' Conference.

Ruth L. Schwartz is the author of four books of poems including a National Poetry Series winner, *Edgewater* (HarperCollins, 2002). Winner of numerous grants and awards including fellowships from the National Endowment for the Arts, the Ohio Arts Council and the Astraea Foundation, she teaches in the MFA program at Ashland University. A lifelong explorer of consciousness and healing, she also holds the PhD in Transpersonal Psychology, has a private healing practice (*HeartMindIntegration.com*) and teaches retreats nationwide. (*TheWriterAsShaman.com*)

Maureen Seaton has authored fourteen poetry collections, solo and collaborative — recently, *Stealth*, with Sam Ace (Chax Press, 2011) and *Sinéad O'Connor and Her Coat of a Thousand Bluebirds*, with Neil de la Flor (Firewheel Editions, 2011), winner of the Sentence Book Award. *Sex Talks to Girls* (University of Wisconsin, 2008), won the Lambda Literary Award for lesbian memoir. Honors include both a Lambda Literary Award and the Audre Lorde Award for lesbian poetry, an National Endowment for the Arts and the Pushcart Prize. (*maureenseaton.com*)

Seni Seneviratne is a poet and creative artist. She has given readings, performances and workshops in the UK, Canada, South Africa, the US and Egypt. Her poetry collections include *The Heart of It* (Peepal Tree Press, 2012) and *Wild Cinnamon and Winter Skin* (Peepal Tree Press, 2007), which has been described as "a virtual master class between covers." In 2010 her poem "Operation Cast Lead" was shortlisted in the Arvon International Poetry Competition.

Elaine Sexton is the author of two collections of poems, *Causeway* (New Issues Poetry & Prose, 2008) and *Sleuth* (New Issues Poetry & Prose, 2003). Her poems, art and book reviews have appeared in journals and anthologies including the *American Poetry Review, Art in America, Poetry, O! the Oprah Magazine* and *IOU, New Writing on Money* (Concord Free Press, 2010). She is a member of the National Book Critics Circle and teaches poetry at the Sarah Lawrence College Writing Institute.

Gregg Shapiro is a Chicago-based entertainment journalist who writes for a variety of regional LGBT outlets. The author of *Protection* (Gival Press, 2008) and the forthcoming *Gregg Shapiro: 77* (Souvenir Spoon), his work has appeared or is forthcoming in literary journals such as *Court Green, Mary: A Literary Quarterly, Apparatus Magazine, Ganymede* and the anthologies *Windy City Queer* (University of Wisconsin Press), *Encounters: Poems about Race, Ethnicity and Identity* (Skinner House Books, 2010) and *Best Gay Poetry 2008* (Lethe Press).

Anne Shaw is the author of *Undertow* (Persea Books, 2007), winner of the Lexi Rudnitsky Poetry Prize. Her work has appeared or is forthcoming in *Harvard Review, Black Warrior Review, Copper Nickel, Drunken Boat* and *New American Writing*. She has also been featured in *Poetry Daily* and *From the Fishhouse*. Her extended experimental poetry project can be found on Twitter (*twitter.com/anneshaw*).

Christopher Soden received the MFA in Poetry from Vermont College in 2005. He is a writer, teacher, lecturer, performer and critic. In 2010 he received a full fellowship to Lambda Literary Foundation's Retreat for Emerging LGBT Voices. In 2007 his performance piece, *Queer Anarchy*, received *Dallas Voice*'s Award for Best Stage Performance. Other honors include WordSpace Board, Dallas Public Library's Distinguished Poets of Dallas, Poetry Society of America's Poetry in Motion Series, President and President Emeritus of The Dallas Poets Community.

Yerra Sugarman is the author of two poetry collections, *The Bag of Broken Glass* (Sheep Meadow Press, 2008) and *Forms of Gone* (Sheep Meadow Press, 2002). She has received a 2011 National Endowment for the Arts Fellowship, a PEN / Joyce Osterweil Poetry Award, a Canada Council Grant, a "Discovery" / *The Nation* Poetry Prize and awards from The Poetry Society of America. Presently, she teaches at Rutgers University and will soon begin the PhD in Literature and Creative Writing at the University of Houston.

Gabriel Sylvian researches Korean same-sex literary history at Seoul National University and actively promotes the translation of same-sex themed works by Korean writers into other languages. Translations include Shin Kyung-Sook's *The Strawberry Field*, which appeared in *Azalea: Journal of Korean Literature & Culture*, and, still in-progress, *Warning at the Station: the Complete Works of Gi Hyeong-Do*.

Atsusuke Tanaka (田中宏輔) is a Japanese poet, born and raised in the ancient capital of Kyoto, where he still lives and works as a high school mathematics teacher. In 1991 the prominent poet Makoto Ōoka identified him in the journal *Yuriika* as one of the major new poetic voices of his generation. Since then, Tanaka has published seven volumes of poetry in Japanese. This is his first translation into English.

Yermiyahu Ahron Taub is the author of three volumes of poetry, *Uncle Feygele* (Plain View Press, 2011), *What Stillness Illuminated / Vos shtilkayt hot baloykhtn* (Parlor Press, 2008; Free Verse Editions series) and *The Insatiable Psalm* (Wind River Press, 2005). He lives in Washington, D.C. (*yataub.net*)

Brian Teare, recipient of poetry fellowships from the National Endowment for the Arts, the MacDowell Colony and the American Antiquarian Society, is the author of *Pleasure* (Ahsahta Press, 2010), *Sight Map* (University of California Press, 2009) and *The Room Where I Was Born* (University of Wisconsin Press, 2003). He has also published the chapbooks *Pilgrim, Transcendental Grammar Crown* and ↑, forthcoming from Pavement Saw Press. An Assistant Professor at Temple University, he lives in Philadelphia, where he makes books by hand for his micropress, Albion Books. (*brianteare.net*)

Daniel Nathan Terry, a former landscaper and horticulturist, is the author of the chapbook, *Waxwings* (Seven Kitchens Press, 2010) and *Capturing the Dead* (NFSPS Press, 2008), which won The Stevens Poetry Prize. His poetry has appeared or is forthcoming in several journals including *New South, Poet Lore, The Spoon River Poetry Review* and *The MacGuffin*. His chapbook, *Days of Dark Miracles*, is forthcoming from *Seven Kitchens Press*. He holds the MFA in Creative Writing / Poetry from UNC-Wilmington. (*danielnathanterry.com*)

Truong Tran is a poet and visual artist. His books include *four letter words* (Apogee Press, 2008), *within the margins* (Apogee Press, 2004), *dust and conscience* (Apogee Press, 2002), winner of the San Francisco Poetry Center Book Prize, *placing the accents* (Apogee Press, 1999) and *The Book of Perceptions* (Kearny Street Workshop, 1999). His art has been exhibited at Intersection for the Arts, Kearny Street Workshop and the California Historical Society. In 2010 he had his first solo exhibition at The Mina Dresden Gallery in San Francisco. He lives and works in San Francisco and is currently the visiting Professor of Poetry at Mills College.

Addie Tsai received the MFA in Poetry from Warren Wilson College. Her work has been published in *NOON: A Journal of the Short Poem, American Letters & Commentary, Forklift, Ohio* and *Yellow as Turmeric, Fragrant as Cloves: A Contemporary Anthology of Asian American Women's Poetry* (Deep Bowl Press, 2008), among others. Her manuscript was semi-finalist in Tupelo Press's 2009 Dorset Prize. She was co-conceiver of Dominic Walsh Dance Theater's production of Victor Frankenstein. She currently teaches Literature and Composition at Houston Community College, where she runs a nationally-known reading series.

Amy Tudor's collection, *A Book of Birds* (Briery Creek Press, 2008), won the Liam Rector First Book Prize in Poetry. She holds both the PhD in Humanities and the MFA in Creative Writing, and she has won grants from both the Kentucky Arts Council and the Virginia Commission for the Arts. A chapbook, *The Professor of Bees*, is forthcoming from Finishing Line Press. She teaches at Bellarmine University and lives in Louisville.

Steve Turtell lives in New York City. His first book, *Heroes and Householders* (Orchard House Press), was published in 2009. His 2001 chapbook, *Letter to Frank O'Hara*, was the 2010 winner of the Rebound Chapbook Prize from Seven Kitchens Press and was reissued with an introduction by Joan Larkin in 2011. He is currently at work on a memoir, *Peter Hujar: Portrait of the Life and Death of a Friendship*.

Megan Volpert is a poet and critic from Chicago who has settled in Atlanta. She holds the MFA in Creative Writing from Louisiana State University and is a high school English teacher as well as a reviewer for *Audible*. *Sonics in Warholia* (Sibling Rivalry Press, forthcoming) is her fourth collection of poems. She has been in competition at the National Poetry Slam and is Co-Director of the Atlanta Queer Literary Festival.

Arisa White, a Cave Canem fellow and MFA graduate from the University of Massachusetts-Amherst, is the author of the poetry chapbook *Disposition for Shininess*. She has published widely and her play *Frigidare* was staged for the 2011 PlayGround Festival at the Berkeley Repertory Theatre (CA). She has also received awards from Squaw Valley Community of Writers, Hedgebrook, Atlantic Center for the Arts, Prague Summer Program, Fine Arts Work Center and Bread Loaf Writers' Conference.

Marvin K. White, author of the Lambda Literary Award-nominated poetry collections *nothin' ugly fly* (RedBone Press, 2004), *last rights* (Redbone Press, 1999) and co-editor of *If We Have To Take Tomorrow* (The Institute for Gay Men's Health, 2006), is a performer, visual artist, community arts organizer, deacon, homemaker and cake baker. He is a Cave Canem fellow, secretary of Fire & Ink and co-founder of B/GLAM. His new duo of poetry collections is *Our Name Be Witness* and *Status* (Redbone, 2011).

Cyril Wong's latest book of poetry is *Satori Blues* (Softblow Press, 2011). He founded the online literary journal *Softblow* (*softblow.org*). He received the Singapore Literature Prize and completed the doctoral degree in English Literature at the National University of Singapore.

Mark Wunderlich is the author of *The Earth Avails*, forthcoming from Graywolf Press, *Voluntary Servitude* (Graywolf Press, 2004) and *The Anchorage* (University of Massachusetts, 1999) which received the Lambda Literary Award. He has received fellowships from the National Endowment for the Arts, the Massachusetts Cultural Council, the Wallace Stegner Fellowship Program at Stanford and the Fine Arts Work Center in Provincetown. He teaches writing and literature at Bennington College and lives in New York's Hudson Valley.

Emanuel Xavier is author of *If Jesus Were Gay & other poems* (Queer Mojo, 2010) and the novel *Christ Like* (Queer Mojo, 2009), as well as the editor of *Me No Habla With Acento: Contemporary Latino Poetry* (El Museo / Rebel Satori Press, 2011). He has been featured on HBO's *Def Poetry* and is the recipient of the Marsha A. Gomez Cultural Heritage Award and a NYC Council Citation. The Equality Forum named him a GLBT Icon for his continued activism and contributions.

Tom Yates won the Poetry Society's Foyle Young Poet of the Year Award twice and was recently mentored under the Jerwood / Arvon Mentoring Scheme for Gifted and Talented Writers. His work has appeared in *Poetry Review* and *The Rialto* and in anthologies including *The Gift: New Writing for the NHS* (Stride Publications, 2002), *Phoenix New Writing* (Heaventree Press, 2003) and *All of These Things Are True and Not True* (CompletelyNovel, 2010). He has also been shortlisted for an Eric Gregory Award.

Crystal Ybarra was raised in California's Central Valley. She is a regular performer at Seattle's *Voices Rising* series and works and organizes for social justice. (*youtube.com/carrionflea*)

c o l l e c t i v e BRIGHTNESS

p u b l i c a t i o n ACKNOWLEDGMENTS

We gratefully acknowledge the poets and presses for granting the reprint permissions to follow:

Franklin Abbott: "Koan" from *Mortal Love: Selected Poems, 1971-1998*. Copyright © 1999 RFD. Reprinted with the permission of the author.

Kazim Ali, "Home" from *Bright Felon*. Copyright © 2009 by Kazim Ali. Reprinted with the permission of Wesleyan University Press, wesleyan.edu/wespress/.

Shirlette Ammons: "Roberta is Working Clergy" from *Matching Skin*. Copyright © 2008 Carolina Wren Press. Reprinted with the permission of the author.

Ari Banias: "Some Kind of We" in *Portable Boog Reader* (2009). Reprinted with the permission of the author.

Ellen Bass: "Pray for Peace" and "God's Grief" from *The Human Line*. Copyright © 2007 Copper Canyon Press. Reprinted with the permission of Copper Canyon Press, coppercanyonpress.org; "God and the G-Spot" from *Mules of Love*. Copyright © 2002 BOA Editions. Reprinted with the permission of BOA Editions, boaeditions.org; "Ode to The God of Atheists" in *The Sun Magazine*.

Jeffery Beam: "St. Jerome in His Study" from *The Golden Legend*. Copyright © 1981 Floating Island Publications. Reprinted with the permission of the author.

Robin Becker: "Quaker Meeting, The Sixties" and "Spiritual Morning" from *All-American Girl*. Copyright © 1996 University of Pittsburgh Press. Reprinted with the permission of University of Pittsburgh Press, upress.pitt.edu.

Dan Bellm: "Brand new" from *Buried Treasure*. Copyright © 1999 Cleveland State University Poetry Center. Reprinted with the permission of the author.

Ahimsa Timoteo Bodhrán: "when i learned praying to be straight was not useful" in *Many Mountains Moving*. Reprinted with the permission of the author.

Ana Božičević: "Death, Is All" in the Poem-A-Day series, American Academy of Poets (2010). Reprinted with the permission of the author.

Elizabeth Bradfield: "Butch Poem 6: A Countertenor Sings Handel's Messiah" from Interpretive Work. Copyright © 2008 Arkoi Books / Red Hen Press. Reprinted with the permission of Arkoi Books / Red Hen Press, redhen.org.

Jericho Brown: "To Be Seen" in *Missouri Review*; "Romans 12:1" in *Iowa Review*. Reprinted with the permission of the author.

Nickole Brown: "Etymology" in *The Broken Plate*. Reprinted with the permission of the author.

Regie Cabico: "Soul Bargaining" in *Bellevue Literary Review*. Reprinted with the permission of the author.

Michelle Cahill: "Durga: A Self Portrait," "Sarasvati's Scribe" and "Two Souls" from *Vishvarupa*. Copyright © 2011 5Islands Press. Reprinted with the permission of 5Islands Press, fiveislandspress.com.

Rafael Campo: "Madonna and Child" from *Diva*. Copyright © 1999 Duke University Press. Reprinted with the permission of Duke University Press, dukeupress.edu.

244

CPSIA information can be obtained at www.ICGtesting.com
Printed in the USA
LVOW090714020612

284361LV00004B/9/P